one bird
stopped
singing

and not
one bird
stopped
singing

Coping with Transition and Loss in Aging

doris moreland jones

Z 48
Jon

UPPER
ROOM BOOKS
NASHVILLE

The Upper Room Web Site: http://www.upperroom.org

Art direction: Michele Wetherbee
Cover design: Laura Beers
Cover photograph: Charles Klein
Interior design and layout: Nancy Cole

First printing: September 1997 (5)

Library of Congress Cataloging-in-Publication Data

Jones, Doris Moreland.
    And not one bird stopped singing : coping with transition and loss in aging / by Doris Moreland Jones.
    p. cm.
    Includes bibliographical references.
    ISBN 0-8358-0815-7 (paper)
    1. Grief—Religious aspects—Christianity. 2. Loss (Psychology)—Religious aspects—Christianity. 3. Life change events—Religious aspects—Christianity. 4. Aging—Religious aspects—Christianity. 5. Aged—Religious life. 6. Consolation. I. Title
BV4905.2.J64 1997   97-11407
248.8'66—dc21   CIP

Printed in the United States of America on acid-free paper

For Harry

*Who was God's good gift
to me and many others*

"Love never ends"

Contents

Introduction

Rarely in life does one line of a poem lodge deep in your being. That is especially true when the line was written by an unknown author and mentioned unceremoniously in a sermon you heard thirty years ago. This is true of the line I chose to entitle my book: despite a calamity I can no longer remember, the poem read, "And not one bird stopped singing." From the moment I heard it until now, I have continued to be intrigued as I see its application to the grief issues that increasingly plague an aging Christian population. In the natural world, wonderful and awful things happen, yet birds continue to sing, the sun to rise and set, the seasons to change. We of the Christian faith need to find such resilience in the face of many losses.

I believe we can. First, though, we must learn to recognize each loss as what it is: valid material for grief. A majority of books focusing on grief consider death, divorce, or the aging process the only occasions for appropriate grieving. I suggest that in any event when we lose something of value, be it a job, a home, a friend, a position, or a physical ability, to find freedom from the loss we must carefully let it go—with thought and feeling. In other words, we must learn to grieve. As we understand and cooperate with the processes required for healthy bereavement, we find we can live life again. Loss is not the end of us. While there is no life without loss, and no loss without pain, no pain can defeat us unless we refuse to deal with it.

This book is about grief in its many forms, and about remedies for recovery. It does not offer quick fixes but guidance for those who feel that looking openly at our bereavement can help us to be all that God created us to be. We come to understand that tears and laughter mix as we strive for balance in our spiritual and emotional formation.

As a pastoral counselor I have worked with grief experiences of various kinds and intensity. I have taught seminars, led worship, preached sermons, and published articles about grief experiences. I am no stranger to grief myself. The death of my much-loved husband has initiated me into the raw pain of personal bereavement and brought a poignancy of feeling that needs expression. I have also faced some loss of lung function, the natural tolls of the aging process, and my mother's diminishment due to Alzheimer's disease. I know well the human tension that denies pious words or stoic acceptance.

And herein we must begin: we need to look at loss and grief head-on. We are indebted to Elisabeth Kubler-Ross, who made us aware of the stages of grief experienced by the dying. I am concerned that some use this knowledge to try to make grief and death orderly, sanitized processes. They are natural; they occur in stages; but they are not neat. Pretending that they are can be evasive or even avoidant behavior in coping with our feelings about loss and death.

As early in our history as the third chapter of Genesis we had difficulty contemplating the reality of death. Eve winked at truth and chose to believe the snake: "You will not die." Since then, death is usually seen as the enemy. To die is defeat. It's a fact many people like to avoid. In my years of hospital ministry, medical personnel talked of "losing a patient" or a patient who "went bad." People did not "die" in this hospital, they "RHC'd" (their "respirations have ceased"). This shorthand language, while technically accurate, may also mask the reality of death.

Loss and death are primary factors of life despite our denial. Losing is a part of receiving. Dying is a part of living. We are in the process of dying from the time of our birth. When I served as a chaplain at Methodist Hospital, Indianapolis, it was the medical facility for the Indianapolis 500. I learned firsthand that while some drivers "hit the wall" or crashed, each individual driver felt he was invincible. Apparently, to return to Genesis, the serpent's voice is heard even at the racetrack, where lives are risked continually. And it is believed.

Yet to the present day, we still see death as the enemy. It is the ultimate loss of control. We are not in charge, and we do not like that. We also dislike the hard work it entails. It is especially hard work when those we love will not give us permission to die. Persons are often sent away to die. They die in hospitals, nursing homes, and away from hometowns and friendly faces. They die without support systems, and often they must feel lonely and isolated. I am aware that we are born alone and die alone, but oh, the comfort of a warm hand or a hug along the last journey. A seminary friend wrote of pushing his wife's hospital bed to a window facing the mountains. He said he held her hand and quoted Psalm 121: "I will lift up my eyes to the hills. . . ." She listened to the end of the Psalm— "The LORD will keep your going out and your coming in from this time on and forevermore"—squeezed his hand, and took her last breath. Who of us would not choose such a warm and peaceful passing?

In order to give this gift to one another in any occurrence of loss or death, we must learn to look it in the face and respond accordingly. I confess, I envy those who can weep and wail. Such thorough release is a great catharsis. We are curiously and wondrously created and not all of us are sufficiently uninhibited to moan and shriek—more's the pity.

Sometimes we may not know we are grieving. We assume grief encompasses only death. Again, I believe we must learn to grieve all the losses of life, and grieve them well. The broken engagement, not making first team, the loss of a job, a long-distance move, a divorce, or the loss of body function are all valid grief material. If we can learn to first recognize our need and prospects for grief, and then be fully human enough to enter the processes grief requires, then we can go on, and work to be all that God created us to be.

We can embrace life and its companion, death, without fear.
We can embrace each other, wherever we are on our journeys.
And we can thrive with the resilience of the bird who never
stops singing.

— DORIS MORELAND JONES

APRIL 1997

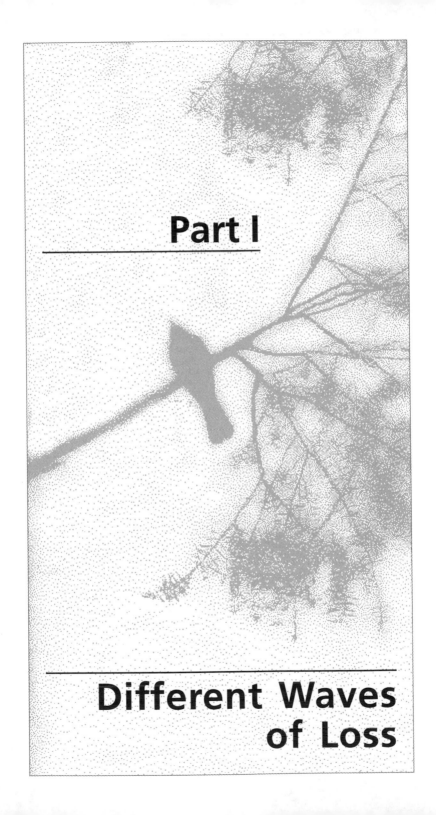

Part I

Different Waves
of Loss

1

Spousal Death: Amputation without Anesthesia

The death of a much-loved spouse calls into question all the certainties of life and faith. What has once been a given is no more. Theological perspectives forged over years of Christian living seem vacuous. The years of formal education in the dual disciplines of theology and counseling do not bring ready answers. The dreary details of death drag on, consuming energy without bringing comfort. The world moves on as if a life-changing event had not occurred. Loneliness is pervasive, reaching deep, ferreting out hidden pain and grief. At bottom of all the pain and darkness are the grief questions: Does God care how I hurt? Is my pain mine alone, or does God hurt as I do?

Grief will not be denied. Grief is a long process, one that we move through a step at a time. As we move, we risk and examine our feelings in the crucible of faith. Such examination takes energy, time, and God's grace.

There is no easy path through this process. It is slow; it is arduous; and the ache goes on though the orderly universe God created moves ahead without noticing. So we must also. Though our progress is slow, it must be always forward reaching.

This requires faith, which cannot be seen, touched, or tasted. Faith muscles, built up over the years by working through other losses, can be trusted. We must be open to experiencing our grief, without hiding in denial. This is a faithing issue. As we hold our questions—Does God care? Is my pain God's?—to the Truth, we experience that "underneath are the everlasting arms." This may seem to call for more faith than we think we have, for those arms are invisible. The wound of our bereavement longs for physical balm.

The Death Event

When my husband, Harry, made a courageous decision to have his second open-heart surgery, the urgency of his condition made this an immediate event. He felt his choice was between risky surgery or confinement to an oxygen tank and limited mobility. It was his decision. He had always embraced life, and in his own way he did it again. He knew well the risks involved, and he exercised the free will that was always so vital to him. I wanted to be a part of that decision—usually we discussed everything together. But after the cardiac catheterization he and his physicians agreed on the surgery. This many months after the event, I wonder if this was his way of sparing me.

Once the surgery was scheduled, the children came from other cities, our pastor, my sister, and our friends all joined me in the early morning vigil. Making the arrangements was so frantic! There was no time for prayers or words of love, just hurried greetings and exchanges of details. In the waiting room, we did only that: we waited and waited. Colleagues, other pastors, and more friends sat with us during the long hours of surgery. Some came and went while others stayed. Strangely enough, we spoke little. Our friends' physical presence said all the necessary words.

We received brief snippets of information, but about six hours into this lengthy process we were asked to move to a private waiting room. We knew this meant bad news. Ignorance would have been bliss, but we who were insiders in the pastoral care department call this the "Bawl Room." We knew we were not being moved for our comfort, but so our tears would not alarm other waiting families.

The renowned surgeon took a break to visit us. He reported grave difficulty in removing my husband from the heart-lung machine. This had been a problem in Harry's first multiple-bypass operation. This was the very fear that encased my own heart in ice. I thought with a taste of bitterness that this was something we should have talked about together beforehand. Then the surgeon told us that the bypass surgery procedure itself was a success—what tragic irony!—then returned to the surgery suite.

We waited in excruciating pain. An hour later they reported that Harry's blood pressure was good and the situation looked hopeful. The next report was that his heart could not sustain beating on its own and he had been placed back on the heart-lung machine: a wild surge of hope, the devastation of despair. This went on hour after hour. Our feelings rose and fell, not like a yo-yo, but more like an elevator that slowly rose only to plummet back down.

Still, I felt the blessing of a roomful of praying companions. The hours dragged by. People's visits ebbed and flowed but always, they assured me, they prayed. Some went to the chapel or another special place to pray. Some prayed aloud with us. Some fasted and prayed. Others called friends or prayer chains asking for intercessory prayer. At one point I slipped to my knees, as if that could have greater impact with God. Cognitively I was well aware that body posture was not an issue, but the ritual was one of desperation.

Those of us who loved Harry prayed without ceasing. All through the long, scary vigil—thirty-nine hours—we prayed. We prayed for healing. We prayed for him to have an awareness of God's presence. We prayed for a miracle. The Holy Spirit interceded with "sighs too deep for words."

Six different times they removed Harry from the heart-lung machine. Each time we prayed with thanksgiving and were filled with new hope. Finally, after enough agonizing hours had passed and our hope dwindled, the children and I agreed that we could not subject his tiring body to any more torture. Other family, doctors, friends, and ministers all agreed.

We went in to make our farewells. Harry was comatose and the medical staff said he could not hear us, but we knew love could transcend. We spoke our affection and we kissed him. We held his cold hand and prayed.

The children went out and I was left alone to say my final words of love. How do you say a forever good-bye? I longed for one last exchange of feelings. Harry could see me across a roomful of people and convey his love in his big brown eyes, but now they were closed. His strong arms had held me in love so many times, but he was immobilized now. His infectious laugh was stilled, his smile wiped away. I held his icy hand and whispered endearments and private words. I wanted him to live so much. I needed him to live. But I gave my beloved husband permission to die. It was the hardest thing I ever had to do.

Once the life supports were removed, death came relatively quickly. Family, friends, coworkers in the hospital, our own internal medicine physician, and many others came to cry with us. The children and I went back to the recovery room—*recovery*; another painful irony—to finalize the death. It was so evident that the essence of Harry had departed. The body remained—swollen, bruised, and battered—but the spirit of Harry had gone home.

Dreary Details of Death

We began the first of the many dreary details of death by signing for his belongings (which still retained the smell of his aftershave lotion), deciding how we were going to get all the cars home from the hospital, one mundane decision after another. We had to pick out a casket. Who cared about shopping for a casket? It seemed strange, after feeling so powerless, to suddenly have so many choices. Thankfully, Harry's sense of humor was evident in the dialogue between our grown children. The humor was healing and freshened our perspective, and thus we could decide.

The goodness of friends supplying our needs with food, caring, flowers, crying with us, or leaving us alone all seemed like the incarnate Christ reaching out to us. So many people came for visitation and the service celebrating Harry's life. The polished walnut wood of the closed casket covered with yellow roses, the congregational singing, the personal anecdotes from all of the ministers, and seeing familiar folks, many of whom had traveled a long distance, gave a sense of God's presence even as we grieved. We wept for ourselves as we celebrated the unique gifts Harry had given to all of us.

Some words heal and others scar. But a hug, the physical presence, the doing without being asked—ah, this was the "balm in Gilead." These soothed the savage wound of our loss. The dreary details of death moved on leaded feet but always there was a hand to hold, a shoulder to cry on, and someone to help, even when I said I did not need help. Of course I did. We all do.

After our children returned to their homes, a friend stayed with me for a week and went with me to Social Security, to probate the will, then to confront one detail after another. Caring people made sure my leaves were raked, the gutters cleaned, and the storm doors put in place. My children called regularly and came whenever they could. Friends and colleagues took me out for brunch, lunch, dinner, and let me verbalize my grief. Despite this comfort, each mail brought another decision and another detail to finalize alone.

Processing Grief

I discovered I could be very grateful and be very depressed at the same time. Grief and gratitude are not mutually exclusive. Grief is so capricious. It comes at unexpected moments and washes over like a black blanket that blocks out the sunshine and smiles. It can be triggered by the melody of a song or the sight of a favorite jacket. Grief leaves us panting for breath. It is fresh and compelling. Grief saps vitality, leaving fatigue in its place.

The death of a much-loved spouse causes the shrinking of the adult self. The loneliness is pervasive, consuming. Spousal death is amputation without anesthesia! A friend wrote recently after the death of her husband, "I know I'll be okay, but I never expected it to hurt this much." "Widow" seemed an ugly word. It is the salt without the pepper—the cup without the saucer. The being less than whole. You feel so numb, yet you hurt so much.

Fear moves in along with loneliness. Grief touches us in our unconscious. Even we of the household of faith feel guilt and despair. We have physical fears, emotional fears, and spiritual fears. We go back to the old theology that we learned as children, which is as ill-fitting now as a dress worn to the senior prom. Sleeping alone is a toothache that covers your entire body that cannot forget when you were a part of another. The darkness becomes a foe and the long nights cover the tears not shed in the light.

Questioning

For the first time in my life I wondered what heaven was like. Before, God said it was good and that was good enough for me. I wondered if Harry could know the pain I was feeling, and if he did, how could it be heaven for him? Did he know and not care? That did not sound good to me either. I read and reread the references to heaven in Scripture. I shared my questions with my pastor-friend and colleague. He let me struggle and then candidly said he did not know what heaven was like, but he was sure that it was better now that Harry was there. The honesty of a real answer was comforting and led me to accept that in the Godness of God I could not under-stand God—for my wisdom is his foolishness (1 Corinthians 3:19). But in faith and trust I can go on to "that house not made with hands." Surely I can trust that heaven is good, even if I do not understand how.

This is the place where many who grieve have questions. Why? Why me? Why my spouse? Where was God? Why did God let this happen to the one I love? Why not So-and-So? Our daughter said shortly after the death of her father, "I can name at least ten people who are wanting to die. Why my daddy?" Our granddaughter said, "We don't have to pay all those hospital bills since Grandpa died, do we?" I had to wonder, why is my mother living when her quality of life is *nil*, and my husband with so much to live for is gone? Again I do not understand. Life is not fair. But I know that God hurts even as I hurt. God does not bring pain, but the price of loving brings pain. As much as it hurts now, I am very grateful for the ability to love, and grateful for the Comforter.

Beginning to Heal

When I found myself crying at dog food commercials on TV, I knew I was depressed. Most anything could provoke tears, and the bouts of uncontrollable crying were heavy to live with. I began to journal and let my thoughts and feelings write themselves out. I was surprised at some of the feelings that surfaced. I knew clinical depression is often due to repressed anger. As I processed this I found some anger that needed to be worked through. I received a hospital bill for over $46,000 for less than thirty-nine hours' hospitalization. I called and asked for an itemized bill. It was a multiple-page document, yet the total of $46,207.07 did not cover lab fees, X rays, or physicians' care. Nor did it cover the previous hospital where Harry was in coronary care, intensive care, and had a cardiac catheterization.

Needing to verbalize my anger I wrote a letter to the chief operating officer of the hospital detailing some of my concerns and complaints, but also citing some very caring people. I received a call inviting me to come and talk about these issues. I went and for about two hours I voiced my anger. I was not raging or hostile, due in large part to my

journaling, and I also had my concerns clearly outlined so I
was coherent. The officer agreed to some changes. When I
left, I no longer felt the anger swirling around inside me.

I also wrote and expressed my strong feelings to the
esteemed cardiac surgeon who performed the bypass surgery.
While the surgery was in process, one of his office staff sought
me out with a document to sign declaring I would pay an
amount above what our insurance would pay. "What coercion!"
I wrote. What choice did I have? No dollar value can ever be
placed on the life of a loved one, but this was rude, insensitive,
and manipulative. There was no response to my letter, yet it
was healing for me to release my feelings in action. It proved
so much healthier than conscripting them to cycle around and
haunt me as depression.

Continued Healing

Immediately following my husband's death I found sleep was
elusive and nights were unbearably long. My appetite vanished
and it seemed food had the taste of cardboard and stuck in my
throat. Reading had usually been a solace but it seemed
difficult to concentrate or too trivial to pursue. A physician
friend gave me a prescription for a light sleeping tablet. I
never took it, but how helpful to know I could. It was an
emergency rip cord that allowed me to hang on. Friends were
so thoughtful to invite me to go various nice places to dine.
The conversation helped the food go past the lump in my
throat. Gradually I began to read again and found my usual
pleasure in being transported by the printed word.

How often when we need to pray so much, we find our
prayer life stymied. I instinctively knew that I had to keep
praying even when it seemed I could not. I made changes so I
could do this. When it seemed I could not offer verbal prayers
I wrote them. I meditated and centered on God. In the early
days I did not praise or ask. I just tried to be faithful to
practice the presence of God, to invite God into my days and

nights and try to sense him. Even today my prayer time involves fewer words and more silence. When I process this I remember how my prayer life has evolved over the years. Obviously, a life-changing event would change my communication with God. I'm still learning to pray, and I guess I will always be an apprentice at it no matter how long I live. It is comforting to know that prayers in all forms are acceptable to God, that God longs for communion with us especially when we are broken.

My work is healing. My clients come in broken, alienated, and hopeless. For many of them life is not worth living. They may be bound in addictive relationships or chained by their own rage or passivity. They need the Balm of Gilead and to be able to experience grace. They have judged themselves more harshly than any jury. Hopefully the incarnate Christ in me can reach out to the incarnate Christ in them. I see my clients go back to school, change vocations, enter into a relationship with God and others. Not every client is a success story, but they do know they were accepted and offered a relationship based on honesty. Yes, my work is healing for others and has meaning for me as well.

Reviewing family rituals was helpful in my healing. I gathered together the pictures of my husband, had some enlarged, some framed, made copies for the children and for friends, and put together some albums of good memories. I watched videos of family occasions and cried and laughed. I reviewed jerky old home movies and slides and it was healing. I sat on the glassed-in porch that was built shortly before Harry's death. Oh, how he loved sitting out among the tree branches and seeing the birds, rabbits, squirrels, and even an occasional beaver. It was healing to sit in his chair and remember.

Giving away clothing and other possessions was something I was sure Harry would want me to do, and as soon as possible. He would not want me to cling to objects in his memory. So his watches went to friends, where I still see them in use. I gave raincoats, outerwear, and sports jackets to whomever they fit. Ties, hats, gloves, colorful shirts, and even shoes found new owners. Harry's collection of Civil War books went to our grandson, who shared this passion with his granddad. Other books went to friends and to the church library. His work bench was filled with tools and I invited family and friends to take their choice. We all kept warm memories in a favorite sweater or shirt, and I distributed these as well. I confess that for awhile I slept with the pajama top Harry had on about fifteen minutes before surgery. It smelled of his aftershave and was comforting. (Sometimes I get on an elevator and catch a whiff of that same fragrance, and for a millisecond I go back in time.)

Changes That Bring Healing

Part of my healing has come from the presence of my daughter, who came to stay with me for a few weeks. We both declared it was only temporary. We tend to be independent and were both leery of giving up our space. To our surprise this change has worked so well that it's become a permanent arrangement. Her son is away at college and she travels in her work. She has a tabby cat that dislikes kennels as much as my lovable, brown-eyed dog does. It is so special to have family, especially when you are very sick—and grief is a form of sickness. On the anniversary of Harry's death we gathered at my son's house. After a delightful meal my son and daughter began to reminisce. Such memories along with many tears and laughter brought immeasurable comfort and joy.

  During the grieving process I found that sometimes being able to reach out to others and be the "helper," not always the "helped," was a good feeling and a healthy change. On any occasion laughter is such a good gift from God, so I laughed as much as I could. Tears are a gift as well. Sometimes they wash out our eyes and make the sight of God clearer.

The sustaining force in my life is God's call. It is the call that requires me to be all that God created me to be, and it is one area in which making no changes brought healing. As a pastoral counselor I see persons with lives strewn with regrets, who always meant to do what they felt God called them to be. Such regret is corrosive and creates a "stuckness" that is not easily displaced. I believe we are all called to be in ministry in a variety of ways, and even in my bereavement I knew that my ministry in counseling was to continue. When a delightful woman was referred to me for counseling because of the unexpected death of her husband, I told her I wasn't sure I could work with her. I agreed to try and if either of us felt it was unworkable I would refer her to another counselor. It was so very therapeutic to struggle with her in her grief. How awesome that God could use my pain to help someone and to help me at the same time. Yes, our responding to God's call will benefit both the receiver and the giver.

An area that did require change, at least for my own sense of well-being, was home security. I had a security monitoring system installed. The motion detectors and the alarms can be another chore, but a comfort when I come in at night alone. The installation of another outdoor automatic security light keeps fears at bay when it gets dark so early. I am more cautious when I park, making sure I am in a lighted space, and I always look in the back seat of my car before getting inside. I have found some of Harry's previous advice rewarding. One dark, foggy morning I was driving to an appointment and took a wrong turn. When I stopped to ascertain my location, about seven young men surrounded my car and began to rock it and say rude things. I was frightened, but thankfully I got away without harm. I said out loud, "All right, I'll get a car phone, Harry." He had urged getting the car phone earlier, but I felt it was not necessary.

Death as a Gift

Henri J. M. Nouwen writes in *Life of the Beloved*:

> Yes, there is such a thing as a good death. We
> ourselves are responsible for the way we die. We
> have to choose between clinging to life in such a
> way that death becomes nothing but a failure, or
> letting go of life in freedom so that we can be
> given to others as a source of hope. This is a
> crucial choice and we have to "work" on that
> choice every day of our lives. Death does not
> have to be our final failure, our final defeat in the
> struggle of life, our unavoidable fate. If our
> deepest human desire is, indeed, to give ourselves
> to others, then we can make our death into a
> final gift. It is so wonderful to see how fruitful
> death is when it is a free gift.[1]

My husband's death is a gift, but I can only receive it as
such if my heart is open. With God's grace I can accept
Harry's death and learn, discover a life on the other side of
grief. There is a temptation to hold on to my grief but why, I
have to ask, would anyone choose the spiritual iciness of such
a state? I'll always regret the brevity of Harry's and my time
together, that we could not grow older side by side. I am
grateful Harry never experienced life alone, or the multitude
of bereavement decisions, or the fear of living without his soul
mate. By dying first he escaped this pain, and letting him go
peacefully was my last gift to him. His gift to me is the
satisfaction that as we lived in love, he died in love. No
hostilities or resentments clouded our union. Death itself
crowns that love with both grief for loss and gratitude for all
the good we knew.

I have painfully accepted that Harry's decision for
surgery was not mine to make. Knowing me so well, he knew

I would try to bring out the difficulties of the previous open-heart surgery. How arrogant for me to assume I was the only one who knew. With grieving has come affirmation. We prayed for healing, and Harry was healed. (How easy it is to demand that God heal in only our way.) Harry has gone to the Church Triumphant. How difficult to accept the realities of life. We question the bad that happens to us, but we never question the good.

The one I loved so dearly died. My world stopped in earth-shattering suddenness, yet not one bird stopped singing. . . . Daylight follows dark, spring follows winter, and life goes on. Couples get on the elevator with me, quarreling about the most trivial things. At parties I hear stories of how unfair spouses can be. Why do they not just enjoy each other? Life is tenuous, so fragile, so unfair in so many ways.

The world goes on. My task is to live life, not to exist. My grief is mine and it is a part of me. My challenge is to remember that in the collage of life it is not the whole, but only a part. While it seems impossible that such a catastrophic event could happen and the world go right on, that is the way life is. Would we really want a world where our grief would silence the very birds of the air?

If I can learn to grieve, to painstakingly go through the process—accept my loss of control, recognize and verbalize my anger, welcome the accompaniment of family and friends, continue to heal others while I myself wait for healing, make necessary changes, receive death as a gift, and acknowledge my dependence in my relationship with God—I will be able to claim the words (however much I push against them) "it is in dying that we live." Then, and only then, have I let go of life so I can live as a source of hope—and find a way to join the birds in singing.

---

1. Henri J. M. Nouwen, *Life of the Beloved* (New York: The Crossroads Publishing Company, 1992), 94-95.

2

Aging Parents: When the Bottom Rail Comes to the Top

My mother has become my latest child. She reared me, teaching me good manners, honesty, and hope. Now, she no longer remembers the date of my birth or my sister's. Where is my petite, neat, beautifully dressed, laughing, happy mother? Her pretty blue eyes are almost sightless. Her hearing is dim, her sense of humor has vanished, and her excellent memory is distorted, leaving her confused and disoriented, and us prematurely and emotionally orphaned.

Several years ago Mother entered a retirement home where she enjoyed dinner in the dining room with peers, seeing old friends who came to preach at chapel, and outings with her family. Later she entered, at this same facility, a new unit for early-stage Alzheimer's patients. She continued to deteriorate in mind and body and now is in the nursing unit.

Previously my mother was hospitable to a fault. She offered food and drink even to drop-in visitors. No matter what they interrupted, she was courteous. Now she shouts to those who knock at the door to her room, "What do you want?" Or sometimes, "Go away!" It sounds so harsh. It is harsh, but if I could barely see and hear, and was totally confused, how would I respond? My expectations for Mother are pre-Alzheimer's and it is so difficult to ratchet them down.

Becoming a Parent to My Parent

Why is it so hard for us to accept our parents' aging? The grief
for me is wrapped around the knowledge that I no longer have
parents, except in name. I have become Mother's parent. I
have her power of attorney. I write her checks, reconcile her
bank statements, and make decisions concerning her finances.

When my father died, theoretically I became an orphan,
for I was then entrusted with the parental care of my mother.
This meant looking out for Mother socially, physically, and
financially. It was a difficult adjustment at the outset. Even
when Mother still remained in her own home and drove her
own car, she was resentful of my sister and me both being out
of town the same weekend. Like many mothers, mine had
always been good at helping us feel bad. Like her mother
before her, she sprang from a shame-based culture, the legacy
of which is guilt. She sprinkled guilt on our cereal and poured
it in our soup, and my daddy affirmed her in this.

At my father's death Mother expected others to do for
her what Daddy always did. Some of this was cultural. Southern
women of my mother's age learned to be helpless and let
others do for them. It was unthinkable for my mother to open
a door, carry her own packages, or put on her coat without
help. This was the way it was as she grew up, and the way it
was in her marriage. My father enabled this behavior. He felt
big and strong, and she felt cared for and protected. My
parents were a set. They belonged together. Clinically we
would say they were enmeshed. My father was a pessimist, my
mother an optimist. I have often wondered if they were this
way at the time of their marriage, or if his pessimism created
her optimism, or the reverse. Either way, taking over for my
father incurred Mother's criticism and my guilt.

Denial, Guilt, and Anger

Once this new relationship had begun, that guilt became an
issue I had to deal with. A few years ago, when Mother lived

at the retirement community, she always carried a handbag wherever she went. Frequently she asked for money. I would ask what she had done with the money I gave her earlier. She always became indignant. She had spent it on "things." Since she lived in a community where all meals, cleaning, and household expenses were paid monthly by check, why did she need money? At first I gave her fifty dollars at a time, but owing to the rapidity of its disappearance, I reduced the amount. In money discussions Mother turned her sweet old blue eyes on me as if I were being mean.

As I returned home, driving the freeway, I suffered guilt. What would my daddy say? He who never denied my mother anything would be so displeased. As the miles went by I realized my guilt is not real guilt, but pseudoguilt. My daughter, a gerontologist, had cited the literature reminding me that the advisable amount is two dollars at a time to a person who is senile. Why is that word so hard to apply to my mother? Is this denial on my part? Of course it is. Am I concerned that this will happen to me? Almost surely. My reaction is so strong it is about myself. Denial and guilt usually hook us at an unconscious level.

So my mind knows this, and knows what I have done is try to make Mother's money last as long as she does. But even healthy actions can give us feelings of dis-ease. The issue really is not money, but meeting parental expectations. We seek parental approval from our earliest time of consciousness. We laugh and they laugh. We cry and they look concerned, or angry, or even put out with us. We bring home a good report card and we are rewarded. They applaud our lead in the school play, celebrate our making the team or first chair in the orchestra. We parade our dates, hoping for parental approval, even when we rebelliously insist we do not care what they think. We, at times, deliberately affront their sense of propriety.

Basically, I realized, I still wanted the parental blessing. My father is dead. I loved him dearly. His death was a blessed relief from cancer. I grieved his death in a good way. I wept, did the ritual cleaning out of his personal effects, did some appropriate personal sharing about his death, and vented my anger. Much of this anger was about the way in which he catered to my mother, creating in her a helplessness that required much attention. This attention was now expected from my sister and myself. Denial, guilt, and anger are all part of the equation when we become parents to our parents. It is natural, and it is process-able; what is required is letting go of the need for parental approval in exchange for the knowledge that I'm doing the best I can.

The Maternal Bond

The bond between a mother and a daughter is a binding and pulling action. It means you can speak critically about her, but no one else can. It is confusing to outsiders as well as to the mother and the daughter. Sons get almost poetic about their mothers, but the relationship with mothers and daughters is more conflicted. Perhaps this relationship is more competitive—competition to look better, to gain favor with the male figure of husband/dad, to be a better cook, to keep a better house, or just to achieve more. We acknowledge and expect competition with sons and fathers, and often try to ignore the more subtle competition in mother/daughter relationships.

Could this be why we grieve so when they no longer compete with us? Is it because we have won by default? Our son took every opportunity to wrestle with his dad during his growing-up years. After his return from Vietnam they only wrestled once. My husband said he knew the moment when Jim could have pinned him—Jim wanted to know he could, but he did not want to do it. Can this be true of the mother/daughter dyad also? We argue to prove our point, but when they have no way to even understand what we are saying, we feel grief. Competition is only fun when you struggle with a worthy opponent, and somehow the mother-daughter bond creates a perfect setting for the match. It is natural to grieve the loss of this gentle sparring.

Early Dementia

My mother was always attractively and appropriately dressed for every occasion. Her complexion was flawless. She had no need to watch weight or count calories; cleanliness and neatness were part of her being. Her sense of style and color was admirable. Imagine our chagrin when we went to pick her up on an extremely hot July day to see her wearing a sweatshirt tucked into some slacks, with her pearls around her neck. The styles were incongruous and the colors were distasteful. Was this our mother?

Due to her condition, my mother not only forgets her enemies but her friends. We may spend what seem like hours explaining who someone is. Just when you think she remembers the ophthalmologist, someone she has known for twenty years, she veers off with a question, "Are those shoes new?" When we can, we laugh. When we are grieving, laughter can be a means of coping.

Mother is critical of what we wear. If we are dressed professionally, she approves, but if we come casual she finds fault. She does this in a series of questions: "Is that a raincoat? Is it new? What color is it? Is it raining? If it is not raining, then why are you wearing a raincoat?" We respond factually, but as her voice becomes louder and more accusing, there is a tendency to become defensive. My sister says she prays on the way to see Mother that she will have patience, only to find it fleeting in Mother's room. Dementia takes many prisoners: the victims themselves and those who love them.

What about Me?

A friend struggling with her aging mother says she finds what my mother does is humorous but fails to see the humor in similar situations with her mother. I am sure self-pity enters this picture. We think, who is doing for me? Why is there no maternal figure to cushion me from the realities of life? Because we have been taught to revere our parental figures, we may withdraw, deciding no one understands what we go through. We may sigh a lot and feel mistreated, but talking with a good friend is more therapeutic. Blessed are you, if you have a listening friend who encourages you to see a long-range picture. It is a special blessing if you can laugh together.

If I look within I can see the gifts I received from my parents that help me cope even with this difficult time. I am both like my mother and father, yet not like them. I like being able to dress well enough in the morning that I don't have to give constant thought to my appearance throughout the day. This is a gift from my mother. I am grateful for a sense of humor, for the ability to laugh with others, and the freedom to not take myself too seriously. My family fostered this virtue. Being tenacious and believing in myself are good gifts from my family of origin, and they help me hang on when I want to give up in grief.

The prejudice I learned and had to painstakingly un-learn, however, was not a good gift. The clarity to know it was problematic was something I had to come up with on my own. The Depression-era mentality that taught my parents a strong work ethic prevented them from learning to play. Playing is still something I must "work" with.

Furthermore, though Sunday school and church were a part of our life from earliest memories, guilt was a regular part of religion. More was said about judgment than joy. My parents emphasized sin, seldom mentioned grace, and taught that depression was a weakness, the result of laziness or ingratitude. Sadly, my parents could not teach us what they did not know.

For all that I lacked growing up, I know I received more than I missed. For one thing, even though she's living, I miss my mother's prayers. I always knew she was praying for my safety, when I led seminars, preached, or taught a workshop. I could feel those prayers. They lifted me up. I counted on them. But one of my griefs concerning my mother's senility is the absence of those prayers. I know she prays, but she doesn't remember the days of the week. How can she pray for me? I take comfort from Romans 8:26: "For we do not know how to pray as we ought, but that very Spirit intercedes with sighs too deep for words." Thus I know I am still covered even though I miss this soul connection with my mother.

Anticipatory Grief

I struggle with why my mother is still living. For the most part, she neither gives nor receives. She eats, sleeps, and forgets. My sister and I have both lost husbands to death, and yet she lives. I recognize the anger as I write this. I know the theology I learned as a child would say I cannot question God, and maybe, just maybe, this is the ultimate sin; not the questioning of God, for I believe God encourages us to struggle with our doubts and ask our questions, but to even be angry with God, and share that anger with God. There is anger in all our most intimate relationships, and by the very grace of God, this is our most intimate relationship. The ultimate sin then is not in questioning or in being angry, but in trying to be God and refusing to accept God's gifts. Even in loss, gifts can be found.

Dementia and senility, forgetfulness, and the return to being children: these are not what we want or need in our parents. We want comfort and nurture, remembrance, and warmth. We grieve for what we had, and for what we no longer can even hope for. We are tolerant of babies who drool and wet their pants. We are not tolerant of this in adults.

What is the difference in our perception? Children will change and grow and later become independent. Our parents will not recoup their memory or their body functions. They will only grow worse. We do not like this. It causes pain and anxiety. The "warehousing" of our parents is indeed a grief issue.

Dealing with My Own Fears

Are our complaints partially due to our own fear of being incapacitated? This could be me! I have no control of this end-part of living. Will my children face this with me? I know what the studies show about the use of the mind, how its constant use can lessen senility. So I read. Study. Take on new challenges. Will it be enough? If I am honest, I know that Einstein and Grandma Moses, known for their brilliance in their older years, are exceptions. Is this a major part of my grief? I have to confess, yes. I grieve for my mother and I grieve for me. I grieve for the bright, proud, beautiful, articulate, caring woman who was my mother. Only no flowers come. No notes, no cards, no condolences—nothing to help me deal with this pitiful, paranoid, petty, confused, dependent, and often unlikable woman who now inhabits her body.

My mother is ninety-two years old and has no quality of life. She has had four falls severe enough to send her to the emergency room by ambulance in the last six months. She no longer eats regular food. She must be dressed. She must be fed. She is in a wheelchair. Often she does not know friends or family. She can be rude and demanding. I write the checks for her care. Each month the list of expenses increases as her bank balance rapidly diminishes. (Many are not aware that Alzheimer's is not covered by insurance.) She gets little if any enjoyment from mail, flowers, candy, or visitors. Some days I am stoic. Other days I am angry. I want to change her. I want to change the situation. I cannot! I must accept her, even as I must accept my own aging.

If I can face my real concerns—and in all honesty they have more to do with me than with my parents—then I can work through my grief. I can face my denial, cry my tears, look at my anxiety, acknowledge my anger, and try to cope with this last part of living. I can try to take care of my own aging body, exercise my brain, accept new challenges, and maintain relationships with a variety of people. (Please, God, help me to be interested, and interesting, to all ages.) With the help of God I can live all my life. I can work and play, cry and laugh, worship and pray, and accept God's grace without feeling sorry for myself.

I long for a formula to live the abundant life. The Psalms are helpful as I repeat cherished verses learned over the years: "Commit your way to the LORD, trust in him, and he will act" (Psalm 37:5). "Wait for the LORD; be strong, and let your heart take courage . . ." (Psalm 27:14). "Happy are those who take refuge in him" (Psalm 34:8).

Frederick Buechner speaks to me in his book *Listening to Your Life*.

Jesus is apt to come, into the very midst of life at its most real and inescapable. Not in a blaze of unearthly light, not in the midst of a sermon, not in the throes of some kind of religious daydream, but . . . at supper time, or walking along a road. This is the element that all the stories about Christ's return to life have in common. . . . He never approached from on high, but always in the midst, in the midst of people, in the midst of real life and the questions that real life asks.[2]

Feeling God's Presence

In rare moments my mother's laugh rings out and her bright blue eyes are dancing and alive. Some days she can distinguish between children and grandchildren, and even remember their names. Yet my children say, "Our grandma is dead." They are right. The very special grandma they loved is no more, and they are often angry at this woman who masquerades as her. My mother would hate to be dependent, messy, and looking as if she were dressed by a committee. Perhaps it is grace that the darkness of Alzheimer's keeps her from knowing her situation. This is a gift in her loss.

My mother has lived faithfully all her life. She deserves better than this. We all do. I pray that even though her mind wanders and she is out of touch with reality, still somehow she can feel the presence of God, whether by hearing an old hymn or a verse of Scripture, by a childhood prayer remembered or the touch of a hand. To be where God is not is hell. I affirm that our loving God is somehow being made known to my little mother. Psalm 71:5, 9, 18 affirms this. "For you, O LORD, are my hope, my trust, O LORD, from my youth. . . . Do not cast me off in the time of old age; do not forsake me when my strength is spent. . . . So even to old age and gray hairs, O God, do not forsake me, until I proclaim your might to all generations to come." Sometimes my mother is so agitated when I go to see her. Recently when I was there she was calm and I recited some of her favorite Scriptures. After 1 Corinthians 13, she said softly, "I know." For a fleeting moment she knew. God's voice had penetrated the clear glass of silence. "Now we see in a mirror dimly, but then we will see face to face" (1 Corinthians 13:12).

When I visit Mother, I embrace her, once again before I leave, and I tell her I love her. A few months ago she would wave and blow me kisses as long as she could see me or my car. I try not to clutch the past so tightly to my chest that it leaves my arms too full to embrace the present. Neither of us is to blame for the situation we find ourselves living. I cannot blame her. But this is not fair. When were we promised that life is always fair?

These words from the apostle Paul give me comfort: "So we do not lose heart. Even though our outer nature is wasting away, our inner nature is being renewed day by day.... For we know that if the earthly tent we live in is destroyed, we have a building from God, a house not made with hands, eternal in the heavens" (2 Corinthians 4:16, 5:1).

Jesus always talks about the kingdom of God in inviting and joyful terms, inspiring excitement about going home. When did I lose that excitement, and substitute fear? Is it the power I want? As I physically grow frail and weak, I can inwardly grow stronger in the grace of God. Even in physical decline I can bear witness to the Spirit of Christ within. I walk in the "valley of the shadow of death" and it is a place where fear and hope clash. How difficult to accept that God could love more than I. How absurd to think otherwise, but how necessary to acknowledge. In the valley, where words fail and human power falls short, I struggle. It is not much of a place for the faithless, and even the faithful falter, stumble, stammer. I realize once again I am the created, not the Creator, and I seek God's presence for comfort.

As I made my attitude adjustment driving on the freeway I was grateful for a God who is a God of all seasons: grief, bewilderment, anger, gratitude, and despair. He is the same. He is there. I affirmed again, "underneath are the everlasting arms." Things are not as they used to be; and one of them is me. Our society has much to learn about Alzheimer's disease. We are confused and angered when confronted by it. It is such a debilitating and expensive disease, but it cannot be beyond the power of God. My mother does not remember how long it is between my visits, but she knows innately that I love her. How much more does she know the presence of her God, who has walked with her for ninety-two years. And the gates of hell will not prevail against such assurance. There will always be things I do not understand, but the power I need belongs to God. God has walked the valley before me, "the pioneer and perfecter of our faith" (Hebrews 12:2). I go on with my hand in the hand of God. Whatever comes, God will be with me, and like the bird, I will not stop singing, for my mother or myself.

---

2. Frederick Buechner, *Listening to Your Life* (New York: HarperCollins Publishers, 1992), 78.

3

Body Loss: I Would Rather Do It Myself

It has been said that if we knew we were dying we might live our lives in a different way. We would take better care of our bodies and be better people—emphasize the spiritual. We often swim in that big river, "De Nile." We ignore our gradual but constant decay. We slough off dead cells, hair, skin, and body waste. We are all actively dying! With selective inattention, we ignore this, choosing to think only of those with a few weeks or months to live as the dying.

Gail Sheehy, in her classic book *Passages*, suggests we may be like lobsters:

> The lobster grows by developing and shedding a series of hard, protective shells. Each time it expands within, the confining shell must be sloughed off. It is left exposed and vulnerable until, in time, a new covering grows to replace the old.
>
> With each passage from one stage of human growth to the next we, too, must shed a protective structure. We are left exposed and vulnerable—but also yeasty and embryonic again, capable of stretching in ways we hadn't known before.[3]

The loss of body function is a trauma. Our faith, heritage, and personality determine our reaction. Stoicism becomes a norm for some, while others weep and wail. There is no "right" way to react to news concerning a decrease in capacity. Usually, though, an initial stage of shock is followed by crying, anger, and denial, though sometimes the sequence varies.

My Body Is Betraying Me

When learning of a serious illness we feel as if our body has betrayed us. Why must I change my lifestyle? Why is my energy depleted? Am I the only one to suffer from one infection after another? Why me? Am I going to die?

To awake in the recovery room to find a part of you has been removed rouses incredible grief. One of my friends found a lump in her breast and immediately saw her doctor. She was scheduled for surgery immediately. She awakened minus a malignant tumor, and her right breast! It happened so rapidly. She had no time to assimilate the gravity of what was occurring. Later, the reality of this loss of herself, as well as her overwhelming anger, caused her great concern. She had played tennis regularly, taken care of herself, and watched her diet. How could this happen? How could God let this happen? Slowly, painfully, she worked out her anger, suffered through radiation and chemotherapy, and recovered both a healthy body and a new, vibrant relationship with God. It was a slow process, and some days filled with despair and depression. My friend has allocated this unwanted event into one of those things that "work together for good" (Romans 8:28).

My husband's first coronary set off an alarm that all was not well. He was grateful to be alive but had justifiable fears as to how his life would change. He asked his physicians: Will I be an invalid? Can I earn a living? Can I be a whole person? Is my sexual life over? Am I facing open-heart surgery? Questions flooded his mind. He wondered if life would ever be the same. Inactivity and confinement led to depression, complicated by his unwillingness to acknowledge "that this could happen to me." He felt bereft at the betrayal of his own body.

A former colleague wrote that after learning that she had cancer, her first wave of emotion was one of futility. Why try? The tears, when they came, were not for the painful procedures that loomed ahead, but for a sense of a loss of vocation. Our identity is often wrapped, as least partially, in what we accomplish. Our titles define us, and a loss of body function can mean the loss of a career move, even the loss of a career.

Dealing with Chronic Illness

Millions of people in the United States suffer from some type of chronic disease. Multiple sclerosis, Parkinson's disease, severe lung disease, diabetes, stroke, and arthritis (including lupus and rheumatoid arthritis) are all chronic illnesses. Emphysema and asthma may also be chronic, along with others. These diseases make permanent change in how life is lived. Although any illness is challenging, most people expect to recover fully and resume life as it was before their illness.

But chronic illness is always present. It is a constant companion both for those personally affected and for their families and coworkers. In spite of this reality, people can live full, meaningful lives. Honesty can help build a good doctor-patient relationship. Patients should tell their doctors about symptoms, what they can and cannot do, as well as what aspects of treatment are—or are not—working. Doctors are not mind readers. Make careful notes of questions and your symptoms before you see your physician.

Chronic illness is not dramatic and some may not see it as life-threatening. Yet the very chronicity itself is like the slow dripping of a faucet. It takes joy from life, no matter if others see it as a minor irritant. Physicians remind patients if chronic illness is not treated in an ongoing way, it can contribute to acute disorders or death.

Community resources and professionals can offer help and support to both the chronically ill person and the family. Extended family, your pastor and your church, support groups, neighbors, and health-care providers are all resources. Reading leaflets from your doctor or a national foundation can help in a less-threatening way as you absorb the reality of your chronicity. Supportive relationships are a major component of successful day-to-day living with the constant companion of chronic illness.

All these things can help you deal with a loss of health or function. But we need more than ample external resources to cope with these challenges; we need to grieve. A great loss feels as if there is a shift, like an earthquake, and you find yourself staggering because everything is off center. Life is the same, but devastatingly not the same. Shadows are longer, people are more distant, and you can't see the sun. It feels as if everything is foreign. You grieve, feel sorry for self, and feel very isolated. Chronic illness requires great courage. Grieving will require working through a variety of feelings, the most unsettling being resentment, depression, and anger.

Resentment, Depression, and Anger

Dismissal from the hospital after my husband's first coronary brought instructions about a spartan diet. We were scared and eager to cooperate. This was before the days of "lite," low-fat, or reduced-calorie items. We were dependent on mounds and mounds of fresh fruit and vegetables. We made it a major emphasis. Cooking, which had always been a pleasure, became a time-consuming chore. Worse still, the eating became as dull and dreary as the preparation. Eating out or at the homes of friends was tedious. We compared choices, and sometimes I did not approve of what he ate. Finally, my husband, with his usual good common sense, shared that he knew I loved him but he did not need another mother. In my anxiety over his heart function I had usurped his free will. Small wonder he grew resentful.

What is it about those we love being sick that causes us to be so frightened we lose our objectivity and our common sense? A friend's child suffered a high fever, followed by seizures. It was a frightening experience for the child and even more so for the parents. Unfortunately, he was reminded by his parents almost daily. Even as he made plans for college, they emphasized a local university, "because you might have another spell." Their overwhelming anxiety runs his life, and recently he has acted out in rebellion. The parents are "wounded" and disbelieving at his natural resentment.

Resentment takes many forms. The medical community notes two categories of patients: those who ignore the seriousness of their illness, and those who focus constantly on their illness. Coronary patients usually fill the latter category; they report blood pressure, heart rate, cholesterol, and triglyceride statistics even without a doctor's inquiry. The former types "forget" medical appointments and even medications. Often they try to outwork and outplay all comers. Both categories of people resent being ill. The former group of patients deny in order to act out their resentment, while the latter patients seek to make others responsible for their discontent and resentment. Both may be denying their mortality, or perhaps, just running away from a frightening and unpleasant diagnosis.

Depression and grief over loss of self-image, our options, and abilities are common. Unresolved grief that leads to depression will usually respond to counseling and/or medication. Generally the key to coping with anger, fear, or depression is to accept the emotions, express them, and work them through. Denial of such strong feelings only represses them, and they often come out inappropriately.

Many of us who grew up in conventional Christian families were taught verbally and nonverbally that we could not get angry. "Nice people do not get angry, and Christian people never get angry" were the words I grew up with. Many of us learned early to stockpile our anger, only to have some little thing provide a trigger, and then we erupted like Mt. St. Helens—making ash of ourselves and those around us. We felt so ashamed for our anger, we immediately started a new stockpile.

When I faced these emotions, I knew clinically how destructive repressed anger could be, but I needed to research how that fit in spiritually. Many persons think the only instance of anger involving Jesus was the cleansing of the temple. Actually, the scene in the temple is an excellent example of rage or hostility, not anger. Anger ignored picks up some bitterness or resentment, and comes spilling forth. Rage, though, can simmer for years. Jesus was in the temple at age twelve and saw the leanness of the masses, and the overstuffed look of the rich. What power does a twelve-year-old have? But when he returned about twenty years later, he overturned the tables of the money-changers, and not only was the temple cleansed, but so was Jesus, as his rage was worked through.

Emotional Release

In a variety of ways we find emotional release from our fears, anxiety, and the feeling that no one else ever felt as we do. Talking with a good friend or your pastor is therapeutic. Just putting our thoughts in words seems to lessen our anxiety. Asking your doctor questions that frightened you in the night can have a calming effect. Tears, as much as we try to avoid them, can be very helpful. Feelings of anger, self-pity, and being hopeless seem to fill our very being. It's easy to succumb to PLOM's disease—you know, Poor Little Ol' Me. Resentment may stalk us, and it is easy to decide no one understands. We risk alienating those who care for us the most.

As I mentioned in the first chapter, journaling is an outlet for me. In times of my own prolonged bouts of illness, I write as soon as I am able. It clears my mind and releases lots of pent-up emotion. Recently I wrote:

Day 13, and counting. I am overwhelmed with bronchial spasms and wheezing. Breathing is such a chore. Being short of breath is not the norm. I was admitted from Emergency to the hospital and placed in ICU. There is an aggressive assault on my body. I.V.'s, oxygen, and constant monitoring exclude sleep. Antibiotics, steroids, theophylline, and other substances pour into my body as if they are force-feeding a python. I am frightened. So many different medicines and so many strange reactions. Am I going to get well? Do they know what they are doing? It's hard to swallow. I hurt all over. I am tired and sick, and sick of being sick.

My journal continues:

Day 18 of bronchitis and pneumonia. Long days and rough nights. I wonder anew, am I going to die? The world will not go away even here in the hospital. People still expect something from you. I am depressed, but understandably it is not what others want. I get messages verbally and non-verbally reminding me what I have to be grateful about. I have a good family, some special friends, an excellent physician, work I love; but I am sick and scared and miss having my husband's warmth and caring. Gratitude cannot wipe out depression.

Later I journal:

Day 23 and I am so grateful to be home. I do not
feel well, but I am able to sleep in my own good
bed. My dog is so glad to see me, and I to see
her. At times, I wondered if I ever would. I am so
tired of focusing on me. I would love to have some
energy. A friend brought lunch—and advice. Do
all feel they must advise the sick? I'm disgusted. I
sound so pitiful and needy. I am lonely. Such a
difference between being alone and being lonely.
I think it must involve choice, and control. I did
not choose to be ill, and I don't like giving up my
choices.

As my chronic obstructive lung disease wore down its
tiresome path, I continued my quest to understand. In a
journal entry much later I wrote:

I know this all sounds so pitiful and needy. Hope
seems so distant and out of my reach. I must
magnify hurts, slights, and disappointments. This
whining, sniveling person is not who I want to
be, and it cannot be what God needs me to be.
At this moment the abundant life seems out of
my reach.

As I look at the loss of my own body function, I see the
times of despair, depression, fear, anxiety, and even self-pity. I
am sure self-pity is a spiritual virus that multiplies rapidly, and
it may be contagious. It is not easy for independents to be
dependent. Nor is it easy for the helper to become the helped.
Fear and despair turn inward and short-circuit our connection
with God. We are then without an anchor. Our self-absorption seemingly carries us farther and farther from the Source
of our being. With no source of power we flounder. When we

are depressed, God seems so far away. Yet journaling can also provide records of God's answers and deliverance:

> I'm grateful for being better, for having some measure of independence again, but I long to be giving rather than just receiving. Reading in Romans about suffering produces endurance. I'm sure if the Israelites had had it so good they wouldn't have followed Moses, and if it was easy, they never would have gone on. An interesting thought—when we push (rebel) against God, we feel the pull of God on our life. This is grace.

Later I wrote:

> Strengthen me, dear God, and help me with my fears, and let me not scare myself as I look too far ahead. I have much to be grateful about. Help me to live my gratitude. Thank you, Lord, for being with me in the "long haul." Now give me patience, or even impatience, as I try to discern your will. Open my mind and my heart and keep me close to you as the source of power and wisdom.

The Burden of Being Dependent

How difficult for independent persons to have to accept dependency. Even a few weeks of not being able to drive where you need to go can be a real frustration. When my mother lost sight in one eye, her ophthalmologist told her she could no longer drive. It was a real grief issue for her. Driving represented independence in her thinking. Intellectually she understood her depth perception was flawed, but emotionally she felt imprisoned. Previously she was the "wheels" for many friends and neighbors. Now she hesitated to call and ask for a ride. When her pastor arranged a ride for her, that she found acceptable.

Transitions may be gentle and almost unnoticed or abrupt and unsettling. Transitions in health are commonly marked by signs of distress, doubt, uncertainty, and upheaval. The unexpectedness and storminess of such transitions result from more than just the movement from one stage or place to another. They may make explicit facts that we have been denying. Leaving the family home and moving into a retirement community may make sense cognitively, but emotionally, physical problems can no longer be denied. We see this in a small way when friends and family will not wear needed glasses, then complain about the dim lights that keep them from reading the menu. How we hate to be dependent!

The book of Exodus reports that the children of Israel complained that they would rather return to the familiar harshness of Egypt than participate in the uncertain wanderings on the way to Canaan. Like these ancient people, we sometimes choose to live restricted lives we know about rather than move into new and unexplored life situations. Perhaps it is knowing that our dream of complete comfort, security, and certainty is only a wish or a longing not to be realized.

Many of us resist the clingyness of others, for we dislike having others dependent on us. But we abhor having to be dependent on others. After being released from the hospital I had a reaction to one of the many medications prescribed. I was dizzy and light-headed and had a fall. For those of us who need some measure of control, this was the absolute humiliation. My daughter insisted that she or loving friends must be with me until this medication had worked its way through my body. How I hated this! I turned again to my journal:

No great thoughts tonight. I am numb. I feel as if all my feelings have been suspended. All my emotions are drained out or perhaps used up. Not good for one who prides herself on being aware of feelings. Stay with me, O God . . . or more realistically, don't let *me* leave *you*. Keep me faithingly close to you, even though I despair.

My fears of being dependent always blended into my fears of not living through what my body was being subjected to on a daily basis. What if I could no longer do the work God called me to? Such fears magnify at an alarming speed. I recorded my feelings.

> Another day, much the same as the day before. Getting better is such hard work. Perhaps it is from being short of breath, or because breathing has been such a consuming task. I read a lot, a variety of books. In reading Faulkner I found this quote: "Grief or nothing. I will take grief." Seems profound. To love and grieve has a purpose, but to have nothing does not. It seems important to admit my fears, to acknowledge my dependency, and to do my best to be faithful. Sickness brings a cloud of despair and a fog of doubt, but I know my Savior lives. Help me to serve, my Lord, even if it is in ways new and untried.

Why Me? Why Not Me?

Body loss may be perceived as minor to one person, but major to the one experiencing the loss. Maybe it is similar in this way to surgery: any surgery is major if it happens to us. A broken finger is a loss of income for a hand model, while hair loss is alarming to a news anchor. We tend to be less accepting of the loss of others. We can be so myopic.

Circumstances and personality cause differing reactions. During graduate school, I welcomed a hysterectomy after months of pain and treatment. The surgery, while not pleasant, was overall a positive event. I could go on with my ministry and my life. A friend had the same surgery and physically healed well. Emotionally she felt less than a woman with the cessation of her menstrual cycle. It was a grief issue for her. Panic, anxiety, and guilt plagued her. She worried she should have prayed for healing or given more money to the church. In a weekend visit she talked of the expectations of others, which conflicted with her own expectations. As she shared, her panic lessened and her anxiety decreased. The removal of her guilt, though, needed more processing. I suggested she talk to her pastor when she returned home and see if she could learn to love herself.

The one thing in life that is certain is change. We welcome new cars and new appliances. New developments in technology are exciting. But rarely do we welcome changes in our body. Again, it may be because we have no choice. A tumor, a growth, a serious illness, or a coronary all come uninvited. The loss of energy, the bodily malfunction cause us pain and hard adjustments. We experience loss of control, and an inability to be in charge. We ask in a variety of ways, why me? Why are my plans upset? Why did this happen to me? I go to church and put in my tithe. I'm not a bad person. There are many people who are not as caring as I am. Why me?

How much we want to be God. We deny it, but we suggest by our attitudes that if we were God, we would do things differently (better). Seeing just our small part of the picture we believe we have all the answers of how life "should be." We become like Job's friends with our naivete and bagful of ready answers. Often we are sincerely wrong in our perceptions. I wonder why we do not question the good things that happen. Scholarships are seen as reward for our hard work. Healthy children are the results of our loving care or good genes. Why do we not question good fortune, as we question why bad things happen to us? Why *not* me? Why *not* my body loss?

Is there a secondary gain in sickness? Do some like to be ill? A client says when she is sick her husband lowers his high and demanding expectations. Another client says illness allows her to catch up on her sleep and her reading. I suggested to these clients some assertiveness training so they might deal openly and honestly with their needs. But is there a secondary gain for us in sickness—not planned, but needed? Can we clarify our goals, take inventory of our lives, and use the inactivity to grow in our relationship with God? If we learn how better to live our lives, to assess our weaknesses and our strengths, and make first-order change in our lives, then hopefully there is enough growth that we can at least consider the question: Why not me? C. S. Lewis says: "God whispers to us in our pleasures, speaks to us in our conscience, but shouts to us in our pain. It is God's megaphone to rouse a deaf world."[4]

Change offers the possibility of growth, of new experiences and learnings, none of which we may recognize as positive and beneficial. Most often this recognition comes only after the event and not during the process.

Growth rarely feels positive at the time. New skin growing over a healing wound may itch and be painful. Cutting so-called wisdom teeth is filled with pain, no wonder teething causes fussy babies. The panic and stress of change can be the soil of creative movement toward deeper, more loving relationships, with oneself, with others, and with God. Whether we face just the gradual daily decay or sudden, devastating change, beyond and through the despair and anguish of body loss there is a reason to hope in the victory of love, and a reason to keep singing.

3. Gail Sheehy, *Passages* (Toronto and Vancouver: Clarke, Irwin & Company Limited, 1974), 20.
4. C. S. Lewis, *The Problem of Pain* (London: Centenary Press, 1940), 81.

4

Growing Older: This Is Not for Cowards

One of the least attractive aspects of aging is the feeling one gets that he or she is often out of step, getting left behind, not quite aware of what is going on. Blessing the aged is recommended but not always accomplished; the "golden years" frequently feel less like a reward or "honor" than a party no one wants to attend. Even the names given to groups of older people are superfluous and ill-fitting. We have classes/ divisions for toddlers, preschool, elementary, middle school, high school, young adults, and adults. These are accurate, descriptive, and normal terms. Contrast them with Golden Agers, Senior Citizens, Keen Agers, and the worst one, Senior Angels (do angels age?).

Shakespeare wrote, "Age, I do abhor thee; youth, I do adore thee." We live in a culture "where youth is couth, and thin is in." Yet we are all aging, despite our denial. There is a period of life when we swallow a knowledge of ourselves and it becomes either good or sour inside and we reflect it in our relationships. I walked behind an older couple as they entered a large medical facility. They were walking hand in hand, seemingly still young and alive in each other's mind (as opposed to merely sharing space, waiting it out). With the gift of memory I remember the hand holding where words were not needed, and Harry and I were comforted by belonging to each other. Age does not have to destroy healthy, positive perceptions of ourselves or others.

Feeling good about ourselves and in control of our lives is tremendously important at any age, but especially so as we grow older, when we may feel besieged by many threats to our well-being. The life that is ours is the one we are living today. There is no other. The more we try to hold on to our illusions of what we think it is or what we think it should be, the less time and energy we have to live it.

Who Is That Older Person?

The way each of us chooses to grow older is as individual as our fingerprints. People seem to age differently in function as well as form. Who of us hasn't attended a class reunion or revisited a church, only to leave remarking upon the ones who had really aged and those who hadn't? As I pass a mirror in the entryway, I am momentarily startled. Who is that looking that way? When I still function as I have for a number of years, why do I look so very different? I have a friend who commented about how she had looked forward to being sixteen, and twenty-one, and even thirty-five, but who looks forward to being sixty years old?

How we look is not the only remarkable symptom of growing older, but it sure runs a close second to anything else, especially for females. The double standard is operative when men look "distinguished" with gray hair, while women look "old." People whisper about how much weight a female has gained while tolerating pot bellies for men. Women wearing clothing designed for youthful figures cause stares, even in resort areas. Men wearing very colorful golf duds, or brief running shorts, do not receive a second glance.

Females are their own worst critics. At a luncheon where I was to speak, I heard more than I wanted to know about aging female bodies. One woman talked at length about the soft "flab" that hangs beneath the arms, precluding the wearing of sleeveless dresses. Another talked of the "shrinking" lip line and the "crepe-like" cheeks she was experiencing. These women remembered their mothers having the same conversation.

Transitions

While some are concerned about graying hair, others are equally perturbed about hair loss. Thinning hair, balding, or total hair loss from nature or chemotherapy can be a trauma. Weight gains are a concern, as our doctors urge us to change our eating habits, reminding us that as we age and lessen physical activity we need less calories. The things we love to eat the best are often not healthy. Paradoxically, the more activity one gives up, the greater the appetite for fats and sugars. Who ever craved a piece of celery or a carrot stick? Our craving tends to run more to chips and chocolate.

Advertisements, the media, and others remind us that these are the "golden years." Any perceived golden glow fades as we adjust to the verities of aging. How can anyone rejoice in diminished hearing, stronger glasses, and cataracts? Hypertension, heart disease, severe arthritis, chronic obstructive lung disease, and a score of other lesser or greater ailments either plague us or the ones we love. I am aware that these are not only the diseases of an aging population, but whatever our maladies, they do seem to stack up.

With diminished capacity we must adapt. Our children bought my husband a combined timer and pill case, so he might remember all his heart medications. Some of his medications had a slowing effect on memory, and as the number of pills and capsules increased it was more troublesome to take each one at the prescribed time. We do not like to be constantly reminded of our illness(es), but as in any loss, we must face the change and grieve it. Then we must accept and act on our need to adapt. Perhaps it is even more painful for one who lives alone or spends the daytime hours alone. Though we fight for independence in small ways as well as large, we are suddenly dependent upon timers and powdery capsules. This is difficult and calls for fresh courage.

Transitions are difficult at any age. We grieve at what we can no longer accomplish and the thought of not being productive. How empty life can be when you feel you have nothing to do that matters, and no one who needs you. This is especially annoying to those of us who are a product of the old Protestant work ethic. We were encouraged to be useful, by the church, in Sunday school, and at home. In this transitional time we must learn new ways to be needed. Join a group whose members call to check on each other daily, a prayer chain that keeps you informed, and learn new ways to pray for your church and family. Each gives us purpose and helps to fill our need to be needed.

Dealing with Our Inner Space

Amidst all the changes of aging, it is helpful to maintain continuity with our pasts. It is important to continue to weave the threads in the patterns of our lives that have been strong and constant. Our faith is just such an ongoing thread in our life. This is a time to direct our energies to our interior space. We can bask in the reassuring presence of God, who gave us life itself and has attended us all the days of our life. "But I trust in you, O LORD; I say, 'you are my God.' My times are in your hand" (Ps. 31:14). What more can we want? Our times are in *his* hand.

This time is an opportunity to prayerfully assess our pasts and come to terms with them. We may have amends to make or be in need of forgiveness. As we look inward we might also find that we need to offer forgiveness. Old wounds from anger or jealousy can fester and send poison through our bodies, much the same as an infection. Bitterness and resentment must be purged. They have no part of living an abundant life. If we find we are tenaciously holding onto these emotions, we must seek help by studying the Scriptures, talking with a pastor, sharing with a good friend, or seeking professional help. As the director of a counseling center in a medical/surgical hospital, I have been asked to see patients who were having a struggle to die. In these cases, how often old animosities, grudges, and the need for forgiveness prevent people from dying a peaceful death. Do they clutch these painful wounds tightly because they fear letting go, because they believe that destructive emotions are better than emptiness? Do we also clutch tightly to our wounds?

Fear, unfortunately, is a part of aging. Will my resources last as long as I live? Am I safe living in the home place? How much pain will I experience before I die? Will I lose my eyesight or my hearing? For many, the biggest fear of all is, will I be dependent? None of us welcomes physical pain, but the emotional pain in being a "responsibility"—what a cold word—can send shivers. Perhaps this is because responsibility is so often talked about in grand language, both legal and religious, but does not seem to be wrapped in love.

"Perfect love casts out fear," the Bible tells us (1 John 4:18), as we look to God, whose love is timeless, whose promise of love lasts forever. It has been said that people do not grow old; people are old when they stop growing. We can confuse doing too much with living. As we age we can make unique contributions that do not require physical strength. If we can continue giving of ourselves, we also can receive graciously. We have much to learn, much to give, and much to receive. Facing our fears can give us power over them, as we discover and process the issues of our own inner space.

Disability and Depression

Growing older is a time when some wallow in self-pity and despair. Most of us have suffered some hardships, "bad luck," disappointments, and griefs. We need to come to terms with the losses we have sustained. If for some reason we have not grieved the loss of spouse, parents, siblings, a child or grandchild, or a close friend, then we must mourn and grieve fully, allowing the time and the needed privacy to move through the necessary processes of grief. It is vital if we are to heal and move on to be all that God created us to be.

Disability, inactivity, anger at being dependent, hopelessness, helplessness, and even feeling worthless are the stuff of depression. The fear of aging thrives on the assumption that I am somehow an exception, and this just should not be happening to me. Aging is a part of living, yet if our resentment of aging is unrealistic we could find ourselves clinically depressed. If you have friends only in your own age group you could be increasing your anxiety concerning your own aging. If you have older friends you can borrow their wisdom and learn their coping skills. With younger friends you can serve as a mentor and learn from the freshness of youth. You will see them struggling with problems that, thankfully, are in the past in your life.

We need to look at guilt when we are talking about disability and depression. So much time is wasted wallowing in guilt. Many of our disabilities cause us to play What If. What if I had never smoked? What if I had not tried to drive twelve hours straight through? What if I had paid attention and had my annual checkup? And you can write your own questions and raise your own What If's. Guilt is an emotion that can become depression if it isn't dealt with. Try to look as honestly as you can at your guilt. Is it your fault? Are you guilty? What can you do to make amends? Whom do you need to be honest with and ask forgiveness of? Do you need to ask God's forgiveness? If you can't work through your guilt by yourself, see your pastor or a counselor. To be able to say aloud your feelings of guilt can be therapeutic. Verbalization has it all over rumination.

The abundant life calls forth the best in us and for us. It requires from us honesty, openness, and willingness to face the good, the bad, and the ugly that live in all of us. It may call for confession, repentance, asking and receiving forgiveness, and looking at our prejudices. Physical disability calls forth all our courage, but emotional disability is the real crippler. We do not get to choose how we are going to die, or when. But we can decide how we are going to live, and the foundation of our lives is our inner space. We must do whatever "housekeeping" is required to make it a clean and uncluttered foundation. Now.

Family Expectations

Family expectations can be a means of control. If nice old ladies are expected to sit in rockers and knit or watch TV, then my family is doomed to disappointment. When that time comes I will work to be as gracious as I can, but I doubt if I ever learn to knit anything bigger than a pot holder.

Four adult children came to see me as a counselor about their dad, who insisted on gardening. He was eighty years old, and in their minds rather frail. I asked them to return and bring their dad with them. He was slight of build but did not appear frail. It was clear they had agreed to his coming so I might "fix" him. He was lively and enthusiastic about organic gardening. He was well read and spoke convincingly. After our meeting, the adult children admitted they had not known what he was doing. His response said they had not listened when he told them. Later he wrote me a thank-you note and asked if he could come in again when he failed to meet the expectations of his family.

Well-meaning family members are often insistent about moving parents, siblings, grandparents, or other family members living alone to a new lifestyle, sometimes far away from friends, church, familiar groceries, physicians, banks, and places where they are accustomed to driving. Pulling up the roots of a mature person can cause him or her not to thrive, or even hasten his or her death. While this is true for a majority of people, others will be delighted because someone is taking care of them and responding to their needs. What feels like love and mothering to one, may feel like smothering and dependency to another. The difference has to do with lifestyle, personality, physical condition, and probably most important of all, how much input the person had regarding the choice.

We need to carefully distinguish among the three age groups of our older population. There are the "young old," the "mid-range old," and the "really old." Who ever thought we would be pleased to be in the group called the "young old"? I suppose everything is relative, and we certainly have many more choices than the "really old." These distinctions became vital with longer life spans, increased mobility, taking better care of physical needs, and more independence in financial matters. When it became clear that my mother had joined the "really old" and could no longer maintain her home, even with my sister and me doing laundry, cooking, cleaning, and driving her where she needed to go, we made inquiries, visited the various retirement options, and chose three of the ones we felt best suited her needs. We showed her pictures and talked of each one and asked her when she wanted to see them. With only three choices, rather than twenty, she quickly made her choice. She needed to feel involved, but not overwhelmed. Despite her diminished eyesight, she had participated in a decision that affected her most.

What Can I Expect from My Church and Community?

Maintaining independence and control over decision making are highly prized rights. But some of the problems inherent in growing older may need more expertise or resources than we possess. We need to take advantage of the services offered in our church and community. It may be when we need a different living situation, transportation, help with yard or house, medical assistance, counseling, or guidance with "those" insurance forms. Ask for the help needed. Consult the yellow pages, or ask your church staff—if they do not know they can find out and get back to you. Asking for help does not brand you a weak or needy person.

Since the influx of older persons is more evident each year, the church must continue to take her role seriously in an ongoing ministry for the aging. No longer will a potluck meal once a month suffice. Nor can we assume the aging want to play dominoes or canasta and be ignored except at the annual gathering of funds. As the church we must not be poor stewards of this resource of prayer power, wisdom, and information. Current statistics show that by the year 2000, more than 60 percent of members in the United Methodist Church will be age fifty and older.[5] This is a startling statistic! But what is even more startling is most people's reaction to this figure. Rather than looking at how this marvelous resource could be utilized, most want to lower the figures somehow by upping the twenty-five-to-thirty-nine-year-old grouping. That would be fine, but it still leaves this older group in a church they have built, where they have paid the bills, often with sacrificial giving, wondering why their church body acts as if they are expendable. The "Boomers" reach fifty this year and are now considered part of the older generation. The prediction is graying "Boomers" will create unprecedented demand for expanded programs in our churches. Will our churches be ready? Is yours?

Can Rituals Help?

As we age, one of the first things we complain about is our memory. We wonder if its slipping is the first stage of Alzheimer's. "Oh, no, I don't want this to happen to me." Sometimes we can make this a self-fulfilling prophecy by focusing on how much we do forget. Even young people forget, but they do not get upset, and we do. Sometimes I reach for a word and it is not there, or a song title, or the name of a person. I have learned that if I do not force it, wait a second without pressuring myself, it rolls up in my memory. Remember, we have lived longer and have more to scroll through as we reach for a name or a title. There are some aids to memory that are worth reading. Check the library (your church library also needs books on memory), self-help books in your favorite bookstore, or ask a friend who never seems to forget, his or her secrets to remembering.

Doing things in order can make life simpler. Make lists of things to be done, such as: call pharmacy, pick up cleaning, write note of condolence to a person in my Sunday school class, go to the bank. Try to have a regular time to write checks and pay bills. I find it easier to have as many bills as possible deducted automatically from my account. You never forget to pay utilities, for your daily paper, or your insurance when your bank manages your due dates. And you receive a statement or receipt every month so you can deduct the amounts from your checking account. Automatic deposits simplify life and are a safety feature we need to utilize. Set physical checkups and dental appointments at regular intervals. Buy a large wall calendar and make notations of appointments and important events. Such calendars show a month at a glance and help us to avoid overscheduling. After all, even good events scheduled too closely can be very tiring.

Some of the rituals we need most to perform involve getting our affairs in order. Make a new will that reflects changes in your life and leaves your resources where you direct. Having a living will can help ensure our choices will be carried out when we can no longer make decisions. I have just had a new living will drafted to reflect some changes in state law, and to declare a health-care surrogate. Talk with your primary physician so he or she is aware of your wishes concerning the end time of your life. Preplanned funerals are something you may also wish to consider. I chose to preplan as a gift to my children. If you have had the experience of going into that room to choose a casket when a loved one died, then you know you will be taking some of the anguish from your family. My children know I think funerals should be at the church rather than at the funeral home, but do they know my choices for Scripture and hymns—and could they remember, if they knew, in a time of grief? This can be prearranged and prepaid and thus not a part of the estate—another gift to your children. To plan ahead is not to be morbid but to be kind. If these essential rituals offend you, talk out your feelings with family and friends.

Integrity Versus Despair

Living life seems to be an art of learning to adapt and adjust to what happens to us. None of us rejoices about problems with our vision or the loss of hearing. A friend laughs about taking a case containing her medications when she travels. She lists hypertension drugs, estrogen, calcium, artificial tears, nose drops, inhalers, something for headaches, a laxative, and arthritis pills if needed. She also puts in her "age-defying" creams, which she jokingly calls her "illusions cream." The laughter and the jokes help her accept the reality. Laughing at ourselves can put issues in perspective.

As we age we change. Some changes we reach out and embrace, while other changes we deny and resist. We must realize, however, that our denial will not reverse the process we're in. A mistake we frequently make as we age is feeling bereft because we have experienced so many losses, and letting that bereavement consume us. The good things in our lives clouded by our sense of loss, we may find ourselves in despair. Then a destructive cycle can begin. We do less, our self-respect declines, our self-confidence fades. If we can develop new interests, new relationships, new skills, and work to overcome our physical problems, we can begin the climb out of despair. It will not be the same as before. Life is not a rerun. Life is a do-it-yourself event with no practice runs.

William Wordsworth says, "The wiser mind mourns less for what age takes away than for what it leaves behind." As older adults we have experience and the beginning of wisdom to deal with life's challenges. I now know how much I do not know. I no longer have to be all-knowing. Integrity is not just a word I use just when it is convenient. Hopefully, integrity marks my actions, and moves me to a state of wholeness.

I make mistakes, but I can admit those mistakes and learn from them. To say "I am sorry" or "I am wrong" does not choke me as much as it did when I was younger and had so much to prove. My moral principles have been tested by life. Not everyone has to agree with me, and I no longer feel it is my God-given right to try to change others. I am profoundly convinced that we are never too old to change, but we need God's help for first-order change in our lives.

To despair is to be without hope. Can we live, really live, without hope—just exist, put one foot in front of the other with one day being much the same as another? Is this the "abundant life" promised by Jesus? It is important for us to accept that God will not do for us what we can do for ourselves. We must breathe deeply, look at the Word God has given, and see what God is calling us to do. Scripture is a unique way through which God addresses us. In Romans 8:24-25, 38-39 we find these words of comfort: "For in hope we were saved. Now hope that is seen is not hope. For who hopes for what is seen? But if we hope for what we do not see, we wait for it with patience. . . . For I am convinced that neither death, nor life, nor angels, nor rulers, nor things present, nor things to come, nor powers, nor height, nor depth, nor anything else in all creation will be able to separate us from the love of God in Christ Jesus our Lord."

Now, there is my hope! All days are not sunny. There are disappointments, griefs, pain, and adjustments. Life does not go my way. I have fears of being incapacitated, of not being productive or useful, of having nothing to do. But in the words of a treasured verse, "I know the one in whom I have put my trust, and I am sure that he is able to guard until that day what I have entrusted to him" (2 Timothy 1:12). In God there is hope and peace—and the ability to keep singing.

5. *The United Methodist Reporter*, July 14, 1995.

5

Death of Dreams: Is God on Sabbatical?

I have a client who was pushed to early retirement, as she says, because of "bottom-line economics." She coped well with the changes this brought to her life. She planned travel, signed up for some classes at the university, and began to volunteer at her church and in civic causes. Then in a routine physical she was diagnosed with cancer. As she tried to deal with radiation and chemotherapy she came back to therapy with me. She struggled with words to describe her feelings. I asked where God was in all that had happened to her. Without hesitation she responded, "God is on sabbatical!"

This response, either verbally or nonverbally, categorizes the feeling and thinking of many Christians. As years pass, possibilities seem to slim, and earlier dreams die, we begin to wonder. Why didn't God do something? Where was God when this happened? Can't we hope for anything—is what we see all we get? Now, if I were God. . . . When such unthinkable tragedies are suddenly front and center, we must find ways to integrate the experience of God's presence into our daily lives. We must find ways to nurture our spirit, for such a need comes from our very depths. A longing fills us to know the all-knowing God and experience his power in seeing dreams come true. Solitude will help us hear the voice that calls out to us, the deep voice within. But solitude is not enough. We need a community that is committed to nurturing as we listen for God to speak. We need a place to share our experiences of God and prayer. We need other people to hope and dream with. And we need to know we are not alone, that others struggle with our same issues.

Must One Be below Age Forty to Dream?

The Scripture talks of dreaming dreams and seeing visions, but unfortunately many of us have given up on either dreams or visions. When did we stop dreaming? Why bother with having a vision? I read somewhere that love has nothing to do with how you feel about the person you think you're in love with, but love has a lot more to do with how someone makes you feel about yourself. We know no one can make us feel any particular way, but being in love enhances our self-esteem, helps us to feel desirable, and gives us the impetus to risk. Could the lack of impetus to risk ourselves also be the cause of our giving up on dreaming? If some of our dreams have gone awry, do we no longer trust or deeply love our God?

The late Erik Erikson, psychoanalyst and author, is best known for his development of the concept of the life cycle. In his work *Childhood and Society*, he named one of the early stages Trust vs. Mistrust. He contended that trust is built early on. We learn to trust through interaction with our parents, then with siblings and friends, and finally with the world around us. As we develop trust, we are fully able to interact with the world, since in trust we take part in the world while we share part of ourselves. For Erikson, this is a religious experience. We might put it in different terms, but the ability to trust is vital in our own relationship with God. God is known in relationship. If we no longer trust God, how can we relate to him? And how can we have a relationship rich enough to produce dreams?

One of the tasks of the church may well be to create a space where people can come and openly tell their stories. It is a sad commentary on the church of Jesus Christ if the church makes no allowance for this means of finding grace and healing. We are not going to reawaken to a new depth of spirituality, to an awareness that there is something deeper within ourselves, and to God who is calling us to a fuller life, if we are surrounded by those who refuse to let us express our doubts or claim our anger; who shut off our so-called negative feelings and demand we "move on the upward way." It is difficult to dream in a dishonest atmosphere.

One of my former clients had been beaten by life circumstances; her parents were killed and she was sent to be reared by an ever positive-thinking relative. Absolutely no negatives were allowed. Questioning was seen as a lack of trust. She was never free to express or work out her grief. When she came to me, she was mired in a world of mistrust and very depressed. She worked long and hard in therapy. Her depression lifted, her creativity increased, and she began interacting with others at work and in the community. She surprised me one day by declaring she had gone to church the day before. I was surprised because she previously had expressed antipathy to anything she deemed religious. I asked her what caused her to go to church. She was hesitant but finally responded, "This church stuff seems to have meaning for you. You have listened to my doubts, allowed me to rail at God, heard my story, and never once told me I couldn't feel that way. So I decided I'd give church a try. You know, I don't understand what happened, but I felt at home. I'm going back next week." Much later she told me she was training to teach Sunday school. As I encouraged her to talk about her decision, she said, "Well, I don't want kids to be as confused as I was. Life has some hard knocks, and is not fair, and I want them to know God loves and cares for them in bad times as well as in good times." Out of her darkness she had birthed a dream: to help children to sustain hope.

God continually calls all of us to new ministry, and this is a good place for dreaming, no matter what your age. We can envision the needed ministries in our sphere. We can dream about how our world can be, and we can be the hands and feet and voices for those ministries. Once we move past our myopic vision we can implement ministry for the deaf, a community where people can tell their stories and not be judged, a ministry to and for the aging, and create a caring community for those who are different. Is this not our commission? How can we go into all the world unless we risk, and with a leap of faith, push to make dreams a reality? While age may limit some of my physical abilities, it cannot limit my ability to dream. Perhaps my role in dream making will be as initiator, overseer, consultant, or visionary. Whatever we contribute, we prove that dreams are stronger than years, and God is not on sabbatical.

Can I Meet God's High Opinion of My Ability to Cope?

One of my ministerial friends who had suffered from a series of mishaps said, "I wish God did not have such a high opinion about my ability to cope." A client told me she had heard all her life that God would not give us any more to bear than we could handle, and then she added, "I believe God has more faith in me than I have in myself." Occasionally someone says, "I can't take any more. I've had it!" It's true—pain and suffering are potential dream killers. What can we do when life stacks up and then tumbles over?

In our twentieth-century theology we are sore put to express a theology of suffering. We do not even like the word. It is easier to blame others. If there is a train wreck or a fire in a multiple-story building, the media pushes frantically to find someone to blame. If there is no one in particular, they blame "human error." It is equally unreasonable to blame oneself for circumstances over which one has no control. We cannot escape suffering. It is inevitable. We can deny, pretend, and try to ignore, but suffering is as real as meat and potatoes.

In the presence of the reality of suffering, healthy religion emphasizes the realities of life and the unbroken aspects of relationships. If we emphasize the forms of love that sustain life, we build a bridge to the future. We accept emotions as healthy, and try to give them the most valid and acceptable channels for expression. We accept there are processes that are part of the natural order, so we do not create illusionary states and retreat into them. Suffering intensifies when we dwell on the pain and anguish it brings. We can confront it with openness and honesty, with the sure knowledge that faith is designed to relate to the real rather than the illusionary. The commitment to truth is so basic that we cannot comfort people by promising what cannot be delivered. We work to affirm the resources of life which provide perspective for those times when life events distort our view. As we strengthen faith and courage, it makes grace available and dreams accessible.

I have an obsessive client who dwells on pain until there is no room for anything else in his life. Each sniffle is the start of pneumonia, and even getting his teeth cleaned is a major event. When his wife could no longer live with his self-absorption, this man spent weeks detailing his anguish over and over. Rather than working through his pain and grief he is in a new relationship which he is certain will be perfect. He is incapable of accepting the normal aspects of emotions and thus is doomed to repeat his illusionary processes throughout his life. Grace is not accessible to this young man.

The philosopher Alfred North Whitehead speaks of those having religion as being "at home in the universe." He is describing a loving relationship that cannot be fractured or broken. Suffering can cause a relationship to bend and sway, yet be restored so it is stronger than before. Basically, what doesn't get us down makes us stronger. This is the true dimension of love. Ultimately, we acquiesce in the face of great grief or pain, turning all over to God, knowing we can do no other. We say with meaning, "Yea, though he slay me, yet will I trust him." If our relationship with God moves us to being at "home in the universe," our suffering, though unwelcome, affirms that whatever our pain, we are not alone. The incarnate Christ in others reaches out to the incarnate Christ in us, the Holy Spirit, the Comforter who dwells within us; ah, this is God not sending suffering but being with us in our pain. We can never go beyond the love and grace of our God. I do not have the answer to suffering, but I have so much more.

Why Doesn't God Answer My Prayers? Where Is God?

Each of us needs the opportunity to walk on "holy ground," that is, ground where no one but we and God meet, as we attempt to discover our identity with God, with each other, with ourselves, and with our fellow pilgrims. The truth can set us free from the pseudoselves we have created to live behind. Our pilgrimage into the wilderness is one of spiritual growth. We are always in process, but never arriving. We begin not in a holy place, or on a mountaintop, but in the wilderness. We pull back, feeling this is no place to begin a pilgrimage. It's too vulnerable, too threatening, and I feel too dependent. I would rather begin where the rich young ruler tried to begin— religiously righteous, financially independent, and socially acceptable.

But what other truth could Christ teach when he began his pilgrimage in a manger, or hidden in a cave, or tempted in the wilderness? And this truth had been declared throughout history. His own nation had to experience the wilderness before they could claim the promised land. David could not be God's own man until he tasted the pits of hell. Elijah was incapable of facing Jezebel, despite his great victory, until he heard the silent voice of God in the wilderness. Still, a wilderness experience does not guarantee our relationship with God. After all, the children of Israel were in the wilderness for four hundred years, and except for a few, it produced more murmuring than discipleship. For some even being in the wilderness causes cynicism, and they cry there is no God, or that

God is dead. The rich young ruler stepped back when Christ told him to get rid of all he had achieved, all he was in charge of, all the things he controlled, and come be his servant. Lose control, welcome the unpredictable, trust in the unbelievable, Christ beckoned. The ruler—and often we—respond, "Come on, you must be kidding." The scriptural account tells us, "and he went away grieving," because he could not let go of that which he controlled, and could not take hold of that over which he had no control.

Do you feel the stirring in your memory of such a time or times? If we are honest, and we can be no other if we hope to plumb the depths of our soul, we too know what it is to hold on desperately to control, even if it is a destructive force. How much we want to be God! Why, oh, why do we feel we know what is needed in our lives and the lives of those we love, more than our God whose essence is love? Our arrogance is a sin we need to acknowledge and confess as we beg forgiveness. This will restore our relationship with the God who answers prayer.

Praying for those we love is as natural as breathing, not just in times of trouble or great joy, but on ordinary days. How much I have come to appreciate an ordinary day. How rare to have the experience of praying for those dear to us without giving instructions to God—no laundry list of our wants and even our demands. How much we need to meditate and pray, and listen to God. I find it helpful to project the image of the one who is on my heart on the blank screen of my meditation. I pray for him or her to feel warmth and light, as peace pervades and strength is available for for the living of these days. Sometimes it is weeks later when the person I prayed for shares a praise for a struggle endured. I am glad to know, but what was most important about my praying was feeling God's presence, staying connected to the Giver of hope and dreams.

Stagnation and Isolation

Is anything less appealing than an August pond with a heavy coat of green slime that shuts out the oxygen and gives the stench of dying? All our senses impel us to turn away from the noxious sight, the rancid smell, as well as the too-quiet sounds of a dying surface. Water is expected to be cool, refreshing, life giving, not that which repulses us. Our personal stagnation is often no more attractive than the scummy summer pond. How does this occur? Of course, none of us plans a life of stagnation. How easy this is to recognize in others, and how difficult to acknowledge within ourselves.

When I decide I can go it alone, then I am on shaky ground. This is not always an obvious decision. Perhaps, because of great pain, we make an unconscious decision not to feel. Unfortunately, we cannot cut off just the bad feelings. Inadvertently, we cut off the good feelings also. We may feel that no one understands, or no one has ever had heartbreak as great as ours. Or sometimes we think it is brave to suffer in silence. Whatever the process of our conscious or unconscious decision making, we end up in the same place: isolated, fearful, silent as the brackish green water, feeling less than alive, and so alone.

As healthy adults we feel ourselves to be lovable, valuable, genuine. We feel unique. And rather than seeing ourselves as the passive victims of our inner and outer worlds, as acted upon, as helpless and weak, we acknowledge ourselves to be the responsible agent and determining force of our lives. We are able to get perspective. We can tolerate ambivalence and not having all the answers. We can begin to transform separate fragments into wholeness by learning to see unifying themes. We seek the company of other thriving people. As adults who are learning to be healthy both physically and spiritually, we can pursue and enjoy pleasure, but we also are able to look at and live through our pain. We learn to distinguish between reality and fantasy, and we are able, for the most part, to accept reality. A sense of reality lets us assess ourselves and the world with relative accuracy. We know God is present. We can come to terms with our own limitations, flaws, and imperfections. It is a time for the process of grieving, for forgiving ourselves and others, and accepting that we were never promised perfect safety or absolute control, just loving, guiding Presence. Would not absolute control be stagnation?

Our very existence is finite. The very self that we have created through so many years of suffering, joy, doubt, and effort will die. Parts of us will endure in our children and grandchildren. Who and what we are will endure in the memories of those who knew us, and hopefully in our work and ministry. Our belief in immortality, in knowing there is a life beyond this life, gives us a sense of continuity. Our isolation grows from our sense of transience. We fear there is no permanence, that we are left and must let go of those we love. In a way, losing is the price we pay for loving, but it is also the source of much of our growth. In confronting the many losses that come into our lives by time and death, we become adept in finding in every stage opportunities for creative transformations. The insight we gain can free us from singing the same old refrain of stagnation and isolation, and create a seed garden for dreams.

Acquiescence and Hope

If only it were as easy to live and learn acquiescence as it is to talk about it. There is nothing simple or easy in learning to turn our will over to God's will. How frequently anger is involved in our acquiescing. In a most ungracious way we mutter, "All right, your will be done, but you will have to help me, Lord. I can't do this by myself." And of course, we can't. We cannot deeply love without being vulnerable to loss. Yet, we cannot become responsible people, connective people, reflective people, a part of the fellowship of believers, without some losing and leaving and letting go. We begin life with loss. We are cast from the womb as sobbing, clinging, helpless babies. Our primary caregiver interposes herself between us and the world, protecting us from overwhelming anxiety. From that time on, even after we reach maturity, we innately expect "someone" to love us enough to meet our needs.

Our basic concern is for wholeness. Wholeness includes the process of reconciling contradictory forces. If we are open to looking at polarities and ambiguities, we can find meaning and purpose. Separation is prevalent in our society and in our lives. Broken relationships bring loneliness and intense solitude. The healing of broken relationships is essential to wholeness. The willingness to listen, to talk about even very painful issues, to remember we do not have a corner on truth, to acquiesce and accept we may never see some concerns in the same way as people we love do can be tiring, confusing, worrisome. But it can also—most importantly—be healing as alienation becomes a thing of the past. John Wesley was adamant that our spiritual formation must be accomplished by all God's people together. Wesley's cells, bands, classes, and societies, which met together several times weekly, practiced the disciplines of confession, confrontation, challenge, and accountability. The intentional focus of concern was on other persons and their needs. In this environment, self and all its demands did not reign. And people were whole.

Hope is the key that opens the door which enables us to enter a new experience of community. It is this hope that enables us to blend the secular and the sacred, and reconcile our will with God's will. With hope we are liberated to be all that God calls us to be. It removes us from the "stuckness" of feeling that life is bad and never will it be otherwise. Hope proclaims to a doubting spirit that death does not have the final word. God does not intend for us to be victims. God's way is to give power to the weak and strength to the power- less. How paradoxical: when we so need our strength, we seem so weak; and when we so desperately need God's presence, God seems on sabbatical!

Hope is nebulous. Hope is not visible. Yet, we must believe and allow God to take charge, and wait for the surprise when we are acquiescent to the Spirit. "My grace is sufficient for you, for power is made perfect in weakness." Out of this power, out of our hope, God calls us to minister in new ways. I well remember my protest when God called me to ministry: "I am not equipped or educated, nor do I have the temperament or desire to be a minister. I have these children and a husband, and a new business to run, and I don't want to move anymore. I don't want to be meek and nice and always agreeable. I do not want to be a minister." But God refused to heed my pleas, reminding me that the called were not always the competent—in their own eyes. Through a process of three earned degrees, clinical training, and internships and residencies, Jesus Christ gave me all authority in heaven and earth to accomplish my ministry. The surprise of the value Jesus places on our lives—this is hope personified!

Integration

It has been said that the loss of parents and grandparents in adult life can serve as a developmental spur, pushing us to become full grown-ups at last, imposing a new maturity. No longer are we known as the daughter or granddaughter of So-and-So. Most of us would gladly forego the gain if we could forego the loss, but we do not have such a sweet option. The choice is what to do with our grief. Do we die when our dreams die? Do we live a half a life? Are we to remain emotionally crippled? Or, in integrity, do we forge, out of our pain and memory, new adaptations? When we grieve well we come painfully to accept the difficult changes loss brings. We work hard to integrate those changes in our very being. We wipe the muck off our shoes, the dust off our lives, our failures, our deceits, our hypocrisies, and come like strangers and exiles to the place where we truly belong. We take the empty place inside ourselves, which we may not be able to name, and we acknowledge we are helpless to save ourselves. Our integration of loss and acquiescence of need reinstate our hope, and thus, our dreams.

The unifying of seemingly opposite tendencies is the grand achievement of life. We strive to integrate our creative self with our destructive self, our feminine self with our masculine self. We work to integrate a separate self that must die alone with a self that craves connection and immortality. We mourn our losses so we may be liberated to creative freedom, growth, development, and the ability to embrace life. I have an older friend who remarks: "Old age is what you're stuck with if you want a long life." A client who fusses about aging and its limitations reminds herself: "Growing older beats any alternative I know about." Laughter is a unifying gift so we can laugh not only at others but at ourselves.

It is important for us to be aware that the stress of unresolved grief may cause physical symptoms. If symptoms occur at the same time as a catastrophic event, the two may well be connected. One way to look at this is to see if there seems to be a clearly evident correlation in time. A sensitive physician referred to me a young man who was suffering from a dermatitis that had resisted all treatment. As we looked at his life to learn the truth that might set him free, he revealed his father had recently died rather suddenly. He professed no deep grief, moving quickly to the inheritance he received from his dad's estate. Interestingly, he shared about his father's frugality and his penny-pinching ways, describing vacations not taken and luxuries denied. He told me he would never get caught in the tightfisted trap that ensnared his dad. Then he began to sob and sob. It seemed his severe dermatitis had started the very day he bought a dashing, expensive, luxury sports car with a part of his inheritance. His work was to integrate his loss, his denial of his father's values, to look at his rebellion, and find a self within he could live with.

When we confront evidence of psychological problems that manifest as maladaptive behavior, neurotic symptoms, and a loss of perspective on life, it is vital for us to be alert to the varied ways unresolved grief shows itself, and to make use of available resources so we can understand both the obvious and obscure ways we employ deep feelings. We need to strengthen ourselves to get through unfinished grief work so we can resume the important tasks of life. Nothing can surpass the value of a creative faith that can see and understand the nature of grief and the value of hope. The "amazing grace" of which we sing is an affirmation of the ever-recurring opportunities of life to renew itself, to move beyond failure, to grow through trial and pain to new perspectives and greater faith. Our responsibility for the way we face life is both a privilege and a challenge. We work to integrate our theological insights with our psychological understanding, knowing we are key in the shaping of our lives.

God's Infinite Creative Power

The death of dreams slams us against an immovable wall where we feel abandoned, alienated, and powerless. The negative seems to be in control and the positives have been pressed out, leaving a flat cardboard cutout of a person. Whether it is death, divorce, the failure of a child, the crashing of long-anticipated goals, or simply the knowledge that there are some things we will never achieve, it brings us to the place where we feel our God has failed us. We have difficulty believing in a God who makes the impossible possible. What is realistically possible for me and my ministry? What if I have to give up my ministry? Must I sell my home with its canopy of evergreens, surrounded by an ever-changing display of holly, roses, mums, and annuals; and what of my raspberry bushes, my pear tree, and the fragrant, show-off apple tree? Must my health compromise the very fabric of my existence and deny my beloved canine friend her own backyard, as well as the joy of racing from window to window to keep her world safe from intruders?

I do not have the answers to these questions, and in some ways I do not even want to know. I almost wish I had a Scarlett O'Hara disposition: "I'll worry about that tomorrow. I don't have to think about that today." But there must be someplace between absolute denial and wanting all the answers. I need to believe in God's creative power and wisdom, and I need to act on that belief. I face God's infinite creative power and wisdom coupled with his promise, "I will not leave you nor forsake you" (Hebrews 13:5), and I have the arrogance to want a road map, a game plan, a recipe, a special attending to my need for knowing. God loves me, even with my doubts and my need for assurance, and nothing is beyond his reach.

An old gospel song says, "Many things about tomorrow I don't seem to understand; but I know who holds tomorrow, and I know who holds my hand."[6] Would a God who called me, sustained me, planted hope and dreams in me, abandon me now, leave me fruitless and my life without meaning because I age and am weak? This I know and affirm: Nothing can separate me from the love of God in Christ Jesus my Lord, not my own fear or the diligent march of years. The promise of infinite creative power and wisdom, even when my trust is at low ebb, or it seems God is on sabbatical—all this is mine in prayer. What more could I need? I do indeed have a song to sing.

---

6. Ira F. Stanphill, "I Know Who Holds Tomorrow." Copyright 1950 by Singspiration Music/ASCAP. All rights reserved. Used by permission of Benson Music Group, Inc.

Part II

Learning to Navigate the Ocean of Grief

6

Processing Grief: From Denial to Guilt

Unless you die very early in life, you will eventually experience bereavement. All cultures have rituals that seek to relieve sorrow and try to give meaning to death. Often these come from a desire to be in control or in charge of death. I once prepared notes for a lecture I entitled "The Problem of Facing Death." When my secretary transcribed my notes, she inadvertently titled the lecture "The Problem of Death"—a slight but important change, as in her mind death became the problem.

The resulting grief is not neat, orderly, or exclusive. It is an individual and highly unique experience. We are all familiar with the traditional stages of grief: denial, guilt, anger, and acceptance. As we process our grief we may be in more than one stage at a time, as well as skip or repeat a stage. Grief is an essential, relentless event. If we deny grief over any loss, it does not go away, but returns at most inopportune times and keeps coming until we face and work through our pain.

This self-study will be helpful as you conduct a dialogue with your inner self seeking your points of pain or despair, noting where tears come, and where you feel angry. It is yours—your feelings, your thoughts, your memories. It is private and only to be shared if/when you are comfortable with sharing. There are no "right" answers. This is a discovery of your inner space, with the wish that truth will set you free. I will give a brief descriptive paragraph of each process, followed by directions and a series of questions. Take as much or as little time as you need. If it is too painful, leave it and come back to it after a while. It is probably best to work through one section at a time. At any rate, do take breaks. You may wish to repeat sections until you feel somewhat renewed and healthier.

Denial: God's Anesthetic

Denial is the earliest process of grief, when all our coping mechanisms seem to be on hold, and our emotions are frozen. It is as if God anesthetizes us from the emotional tearing of life's fabric. Our minds seem to be in slow motion as we ask and re-ask for details. Our decision-making ability is *nil*, and we have trouble focusing during this time of shock anesthetic. Unfortunately, the quick fix of tranquilizers denies us this normal reaction of grief and may extend the denial an unhealthy length of time. Denial is real and needed for a while as we accept the hard truth of our loss. It is easy to deny that a marriage is over, a child is in trouble, or we did not get assigned the church of our choice. To continue to deny that one we loved, or something else significant, is gone may be a temptation, but it only increases the recovery time. At times one leaves denial only to return to it at a later stressful time. If the cocoon of denial is too comfortable, there is a tendency to linger, which retards the process of working through grief and getting on with living.

Find a private place with a comfortable chair and take with you a pad of paper and a pen or pencil. This is a good time to let the answering machine field your calls. Keep the temperature comfortable, and place a box of tissues within easy reach. Breathe a prayer as you ask the Lord to be with you.

Where were you when you learned of your loss? What were you doing? Can you picture the environment? Do you remember any sounds? Were there any smells you recall? Who told you of your loss? What feelings are you in touch with—sadness, pain, anger, despair, lack of reality, numbness?

Stay with your feelings, write them down, and try not to be too concerned even if your feelings are different from what you expected. Remember, feelings are neither right nor wrong. Our feelings just are, and we choose what we do with them. The choice is ours. This is a time to remember all that was blocked when we first learned of our loss.

Who was helpful when you experienced this time of sorrow? Whom were you anxious to tell? Were you disappointed at the actions or reactions of those you shared with? Do you remember inane or stupid remarks made by well-meaning friends or family? Were you bothered by people asking what they could do to help, rather than helping?

Where was God in all this? Did you feel alienated and alone? When did God's presence become a reality? Were you able to pray, or did you rejoice in others praying for you? Did you wonder why this happened to you when you worked so hard and tried to live right? Did you ask, "Why did this happen? Why did this happen now?"

Do not feel pressured because you have no conclusive answers. This is an internal dialogue, and you are on a journey to know yourself. It is not easy but it is so very worthwhile.

Emotional Release: Thawing of a Frozen Heart

Emotional release takes many forms, although the most usual seems to be tears—silent tears, great shaking sobs, hiccuping crying, or even a runny nose. But not everyone cries. Some walk the floor, rake leaves, do laundry, or wring their hands. I had a client who walked mile after mile to release emotional tension, and it was many weeks before tears came. This emotional "letting down" may happen later rather than sooner. Family-of-origin training that is caught rather than taught is often responsible for the form of our emotional release. A comfortable silence, an embrace, the willingness to listen without watching the clock encourages release, especially since we usually are more afraid of our own emotions than the emotions of others. Feelings are important, and facts can come later. Crying itself is comforting. Grief is the spiritual reaction to being separated from that which had meaning for us. This process of grief is a system's movement toward wholeness.

Now for your inner dialogue. Use your pad of paper and return to your comfortable place. Pray that God will be with you in this process; you are ready to grow and learn from what has happened to your life.

Where were you when you first felt the emotional release due to the enormity of your grief? Were you alone? Did anyone tell you not to cry? Did anyone hint that your tears might signify a lack of faith? Were you told you could not feel the way you felt?

As you were crying, did anyone use this as an opportunity to tell of his or her own grief experience? This is insensitive and not helpful, even when it is meant otherwise, and it is all right for you to feel resentful.

Are you feeling sadness, relief, misunderstood, fear, anger, or numb? Please write down your feelings, and try not to be concerned if some of your feelings surprise you.

Do you feel you were rushed to return to work or school? It is reasonable to feel that a three-day leave is extremely unfair when you've lost someone you loved. Furthermore, it is natural to feel you needed time to heal even if you lost something other than a person. All significant loss calls for grieving, be it a home, a pet, a promotion, or a bodily function.

Do you feel pressured to not cry in front of other people? Do you sense your tears make them uncomfortable? Who lets you cry and encourages your emotional release?

Were you told to count your blessings when you cried or stomped your foot? Did anyone dismiss or minimize your pain? Were you told of others who were having a bad time? Did you feel like crying out that your circuits were overloaded, and you couldn't take anymore in at this time?

Relax, breathe deeply, note any new feeling that came up as you looked inward. Give yourself a hug, and try not to be too punishing if no new insight was received. This is a long journey, not completed without a struggle.

Depression: Feeling Helpless, Hopeless, and Worthless

This is one of the longest lasting and most repeated of the processes of grief. It's when we feel no one understands or no one ever suffered as we. Self-pity is a spiritual virus that reinfects us again and again. We may go back to denial as we fantasize about happier times. Everything seems hopeless, we are helpless to change anything in our lives, and it seems as if we are without worth and most everyone would be better off if we were not around. We have no interest in anything as normal events have ceased to give pleasure. Eating is a chore where we can't taste or swallow, or where we comfort ourselves with fats and sugars. Sleeping is an issue with early morning awakening, insomnia, or a desire to oversleep to escape. The helpless/hopeless/worthless stuff is the very meat of depression, and it keeps us from making any attempt to help ourselves. It seems as if all joy has been sucked from life, and isolation becomes a lifestyle. God seems to be so far away just when we need our God the very most. Our prayers seem to fall short, and no one can know our misery, not even God.

Now go to your comfortable, private space where you have assurance you will not be disturbed. If you find yourself falling asleep, try for a place with more light and stimulation. Sleep may be a withdrawal from the world and could perpetuate your grief process. Have tissues, paper, and pen at hand, and breathe a prayer for the presence of our living Lord.

How long have you been feeling sorry for yourself? Are you put out that you can't seem to get past this hurdle? How long have you felt that life is not worth living? Do you find yourself sighing often, especially when you turn down an invitation? Is everything just too much trouble?

Are you sleeping your normal schedule? How has your appetite changed since you have been grieving? Do you find yourself in tears during commercials or when you hear the news? Do you have trouble making and following through with a decision? Are you always fatigued? Is apathy a way of life? Have you lost your desire to compete, even with yourself?

Do you feel friends and family are disgusted with you and think you are not trying to get through your pain? Do you no longer care what they think? Is your perception of life a dark hole, where you lie all alone in a fetal position? Are you frightened, complacent, sad, worried, angry, or on automatic pilot?

With whom are you talking with about your concerns? How angry are you at this event in your life? Are you feeling guilt about what you did or did not do? Have you talked with your physician, your pastor, a trusted friend? Do you need to talk with a pastoral counselor to get through this time?

Where is God in all this? Do you feel God is on vacation and you are left to fend for yourself? Do you feel anger or just feel that you are unworthy of God's attention? Do you need to call a friend to pray for you and verbalize your needs out loud? Do you need to be assured that it is all right to seek help? (*It is.*)

Are you told repeatedly to count your blessings, with the distinct impression that if you were grateful enough you would not be depressed? Remember, you can be very grateful and very depressed. These emotions are not mutually exclusive. Has anyone suggested you should "get hold of yourself"? (Isn't that an inappropriate remark! Where are the handles to take hold of self?)

This is a tiring process. Try to take a walk, get some fresh air, do some aerobics. Write down any new insights, or even tentative insights. Be kind to new thoughts and feelings and let them be until you accept or reject them. You may need to review what you felt more than once, and some of these feelings will be different from what you expected. That is all right. God likes variety and difference and will be with you in this pilgrimage.

Physical Symptoms: I Am So Tired!

Fatigue, irritability, weakness, anxiety, and pains without apparent physical causes are part and parcel of this process of grief. Exhaustion and feeling as if you have a weight on your chest are part of the visceral reaction that is most often expressed with the words, "I am so tired." A depressed immune system allows headaches, backaches, colds, and upsets in the gastrointestinal tract. Despite our being so tired, sleep eludes us. In the middle of the night each pain is major and fear pushes sleep even further away. As the cycle of fear and cognition repeats we have the very antithesis of rest. In this process of grief we can become very difficult to love. As we become wrapped in ourselves we become less attractive to others and are frequently excluded. It is a self-fulfilling prophecy. We have to break the cycle, recognizing grief as a controlling, consuming emotion that we must work through.

Now, please go to your special place of retreat, where you have arranged for privacy and space. Have paper, pen, tissues at hand, and the answering machine ready to collect your calls. Meditate briefly on God's care for you and ask for his presence as you begin to search your inner self.

How long have you been feeling tired, worn out, apathetic? Was this evident before this loss? When was your last physical checkup? Are you taking any sedatives or tranquilizers?

How much exercise do you participate in regularly? Are you napping during the day? Do you sleep in your chair? Do you stay up later, hoping to go to sleep easier? Do you arise at

a regular time, even if you went to sleep later? Are you consuming any caffeine after 5 P.M.? Are you self-medicating with
alcohol? How much are you smoking?

What are you reading? Are you challenged by crossword
puzzles or the like? Do you read the daily newspaper or watch
local and national news programs? Have you disagreed with any
person since your loss? Why not? Are you usually so passive?

Have you invited anyone into your home to share a
meal? Are you eating fast food and take-out? Does everything
you consume consist of either sugar or fat? Do you feel you are
nondeserving of a regular meal? Are you punishing yourself?
Why? The loss you have sustained is no excuse for martyr-
dom. Are you attempting to atone for things that were lacking
in the relationship you lost?

Now, take a deep breath and see if the sun is shining or
the moon is glowing. Listen to the sounds of life. Love your
pet if you have one, connect with family, call a friend, determine to take one concrete step out of your malaise. Plan one
new thing for tomorrow, thanking God for the opportunity to
participate in life.

Panic and Anxiety: I Can't Go On!

There are twelve recognized symptoms of panic: pounding
heart, breathing difficulty, tingling in fingers or feet, tightness
of the chest, overwhelming anxiety, a smothering sensation,
faintness, sweating, trembling, hot or cold flashes, a sense of
unreality, and a fear of dying. It is small wonder in this process
of grief we exclaim, "I can't go on like this!" You may feel
anger at this point because it seems you've been left to suffer.
This aspect of grief can come anytime and reappear frequently. It may be a "fight or flight" response brought on by
being overstressed with decisions. Hyperventilation and/or
heart palpitations may be evident. This process of grief seems
to come when we are least able to cope and less able to
recognize what is happening to us. It may feel as if your feet

are stuck in a morass of molasses, and paranoia can reign. Anxiety seems rampant and your logical self is nowhere to be found. Your sense of any control over your own life seems null and void. It is a scary time.

Pull apart with some privacy, but you may feel the need to have a friend or family member standing by, at least by the phone. If you become tense or anxious, or feel panic symptoms, call your backup person. This may be the time to contact your pastor, priest, or rabbi, or to enter into a good counseling relationship. Those who love us grow tired and confused as to how to help. An objective, caring professional can be so helpful in dealing with the crippling effects of panic and anxiety. Panic does give way to action, even the light of hope.

If you have attempted to look at your panic and anxiety before, it may be helpful to take a brisk walk before you seek your private inner space. Gather your usual comforts around you and begin with a session of tensing and relaxing your muscles. Tense as tight as you can for a count of eight and then relax as much as possible for another count of eight. Focus on your breathing by taking in as deep a breath as you can, holding it for a count of five, then exhaling very slowly.

Look back at your life and see when you have previously felt panic symptoms. Have you ever felt trapped by your own anxiety? Does being anxious frequently keep you from doing what you want in life? Do any family members suffer with either panic or anxiety? Are you ashamed of these feelings? Do you regard them as a weakness? Why?

What calms your anxieties? Who has been helpful in relieving your panic? Can you concentrate on remembering something difficult and/or challenging to change the focus from self to a larger world? (I have a client who tries to whistle "The William Tell Overture" when he is panicked. He says he cannot always remember, but the process puts a "stop sign" on his anxiety.)

There is time another day for more recalling. Have a cool drink, wash your face in cold water, praise yourself for having the courage to look at your life. If you have gained any insight, write it down, but do not look too hard for obscure meaning. Insight is often slow in coming. Folks who get instant results are probably in the minority. Often insight comes as we walk the dog, drive, or make the bed. It cannot be forced.

Put your hand in the hand of God. Try to relax. Work at being grateful, and try to do one thing that is separate from your grief for someone else. Sing the doxology and mean it, if not for your life then for the life of someone you love.

Guilt: Real Guilt or Pseudoguilt

Guilt may be an initial reaction or come late in the experience of grief. The most loving relationship broken by death, divorce, or disaster will create some guilt. We need to be concerned when we wonder if we could have changed the grief event by our actions of omission or commission. Real guilt must be acknowledged, and in the recognition healing can begin. If we have slandered or been dishonest we must make amends. Be aware that much of the guilt that plagues us is not real guilt but pseudoguilt, as I mentioned in chapter 2. It is important to discern the difference. Pseudoguilt would have us second-guess every interpersonal transaction. It is easy to "should" ourselves until we are black and blue. In almost all cases we wish we had expressed, at least once more, our love, or left unsaid unkind words or actions. Or perhaps we feel guilt because of placing our own concerns first or because we were too busy or preoccupied. Since we are so very human, there is no way we can be guilt-free. The strong, invasive feeling that we could have changed events by our intervention always gives us more power than we truly have.

It's time to retreat to your private sanctuary to look at how you process guilt. Since we are looking at the depth and width of our innermost selves, we need utmost privacy. Be as comfortable as you can with a good chair, optimum environment and temperature, privacy and quiet, and your usual tissues, pad of paper, and a pen. Breathe a prayer for God's vision as you enter this quest.

What one message would you most like to deliver to that one who is no longer in your life? Would it be words of love, of apology for not seeing more clearly, or thanksgiving for the relationship you enjoyed? Do you need forgiveness from that person? Is there restitution you need to make? Do you need forgiveness from God? Could you be feeling God is blaming you? When did this first come in your mind?

Are you angry with the one you have lost? Could you write a letter to this person talking about your guilt and anger? Are you asking "Why?" or "Why me?" If you had one phone call to make in an effort to resolve your guilt, whom would you call? What would you say? Can you write your letter or role-play your phone call? What keeps you from doing this?

Thinking of the one you lost, do you feel solely responsible because you did not insist he/she go to the emergency room or see the doctor sooner? Do you blame yourself because you did not watch someone's diet more closely, so he/she gained weight? Or are your regrets involved with your own weight gain, with your family-of-origin involvement, or your crucial career move? Has everything that has happened been your fault? Are you really so powerful? Be honest with yourself as you look inward.

Do you ruminate about lost opportunities, or play a game of What If? Does it feel like the whole world is on your shoulders? Where did you learn this super-responsibility? Who else in your family is this way—to the point of frenzy? Are you really den mother of the universe?

Where is God in this picture? Could you have shut out God in an attempt to be in control? Do you enjoy feeling guilty? Is it a comfortable place where you spend time frequently? What needs to happen for you to forgive yourself, and ask God for forgiveness?

This is a heavy process and I know you are weary. Arise,

stretch, reach out to touch a flower or a plant, note the texture of the day, the color of the sky; and look honestly inside as you see yourself in God's world. Give up your guilt, drop by drop, until you find the forgiveness and love you crave and need. Write down what you have learned, for we all have selective inattention when it comes to our own processes. Since guilt is such a heavy, cumbersome, noxious part of grief, be aware you may return to this process again and again in order to purge the corrosive elements. Real grief is a clear signal to change our way, and must be heeded, for I am certain the "abundant life" promised by Jesus Christ does not include a lifetime of guilt.

Earlier I mentioned a lecture I wrote called "The Problem of Facing Death." The problem of facing facing grief is that it is such an overwhelming task. It must be broken into stages and then into steps. As we cooperate with the process of grief, we find the ability to keep singing—a few notes at a time.

More Processing of Grief: From Anger to Acceptance

As we move on through the processes of grief we know that each grief is different. Close-range grief is painful and laborious. The empathy we feel from others is a willingness to enter our pain, not in an up/down sense, but in an act of being with us, even when we are unloving to be around. Real grief is never addressed to "Occupant." It is our burden and a responsibility of our most personal space. The most intimate part of us is revealed in our grieving. The rational, cognitive part of us that we usually revere takes a holiday when we are immersed in the process of a grief event. Tears, sobbing, and loss of control are acceptable in a world where such behavior is usually abhorred. How vital to our well-being to work through the verities of our grief. Research documents that unresolved grief leads to a variety of psychosomatic ailments. Acting-out behavior and unwise personal decisions can be a consequence of not exploring our internal spaces. Grief addressed and worked through gives us a depth of understanding not known before, but it is a long and arduous task.

Edgar Jackson wrote *The Many Faces of Grief* over twenty years ago, and it has been reprinted numerous times. He felt that pastors tried to spiritualize death, morticians generalized it, and physicians wanted to sedate the grieved. All of these techniques encourage escape from emotions. Our culture has little patience with grief. We are urged forward, to "get on with life." At weddings we are surrounded with well-wishers and advice-givers. At birth we are inundated with gifts, accompanied by a plethora of congratulations and unsolicited advice. We always celebrate graduation and promotions, but modern support systems are most peculiar. At a time when we are finding communication almost impossible, society withdraws in embarrassed silence. Often we are regulated to a vacuum, without a sounding board of colleagues.

Most of us are naively unprepared to work our way through this dimension, especially when we are trying to navigate both the practical and emotional problems of loss. How difficult to find balance. It is easier to ride off in all directions, since we are without a trail or a road map, and most people are content to let us alone, as long as we do not disrupt their lives. This self-study will, hopefully, serve as a compass, a guide star if you wish, as we make our way through the murky and uncharted waters of grief.

Remember, this self-study is private and personal, not to share unless you are comfortable in sharing. There are no right or wrong answers. This is a personal journey of your process of grieving, looking inward for the truth that sets you free. Note where you cry, feel embarrassed, chagrined, or worried. I will again give you a series of questions and directions, preceded by a brief descriptive passage of each process. Take as much or as little time as feels right to you, but if you find this too painful, let it be until another day. Repeat sections as you feel necessary.

Anger: Not Me?

This is the stage of grief that we most frequently try to bypass, yet it is a well-known phenomena. We can accept tears, depression, anxiety, and even denial, but not hostility or rage. This may explain why this stage of grief is often late in coming. Some feel they have finished their grief process only to find they are blindsided by hostility. There is ambivalence in all love relationships as rage exists right alongside affection and tenderness. This may take many forms: anger at one who is gone, anger at doctors or hospitals, anger at an ex-spouse, anger at an employer for requiring a long-distance move, anger with parents for not taking better care of themselves, rage for the poor choices made by our children, anger at government or insurance regulations, or anger with the church, pastor, or God. Until we realize our rage and hostility and express it in appropriate ways, we are helpless to work it through. We become victims of it.

Our anger with God can be a white-hot fire, but we are "too nice" to give vent to our feelings since we have a perverted notion that we need to protect God. How absurd! As if God needed protection from us. If we can be honest with our own feelings and make a careful assessment, looking for a healthy response to our hostility, we can find release and peace. This is not a "dumping game" but a time of truth and honesty where we acknowledge our anger and see what is underneath it. Our Creator is always with us in our suffering and hurts even as we hurt. Unexpressed rage, whether it is directed at God or persons, cycles around and can become depression, or seek an outlet in physical illness.

Expressions of anger are frequently oblique. When we protest the absurdity of an existence that flings those we love onto earth only to sweep them away again, these protestations are expression of anger toward God. Not going to church, not praying, not giving tithes and offerings can all be acts of hostility. Withdrawal from all normal activities, acting-out behavior, or substance abuse may also be passive-aggressive ways of showing anger or rage. Be mindful that hostility is anger under pressure, and to soothe it we must look to the initial impetus of the anger.

Once again seek out a very private, comfortable place. This is personal business of the utmost importance. Place your needed pad, pen, and tissues close at hand, and maybe add a glass of water or fruit juice. Breathe a prayer for truth and direction as you sit quietly waiting.

Think of your loss, feel your grief and despair. What

one thing would you change if you could? Are you enraged because you had no input into the decision process that produced this loss? Did you feel left out or diminished by not having an active role? Do you wonder, why was I not asked? Were they afraid I would take a broader outlook at the problem?

Are any of these your thoughts: Why didn't God save this one I loved? Where was God when this happened? If I were God, I would have treated this in a different way. Oh, God, I don't think you have been fair. And I prayed, God, oh, how I prayed, and what did you do? Nothing! I want a recount, a new deal, another chance. I know one thing, Lord; I am angry with you and I am not going to deny it anymore.

What keeps you from getting on with your life? Do you feel you've been stuck in the same place for weeks? Does it seem you are caught in a trap with no one to release you? Do you wonder, why me? What do I need to do? What is it that keeps me from doing what must be done? Do you wish you could rail out at someone or dump your rage on some poor guy who puts gas in your car or forgets to bring your newspaper? What can you safely kick? Can you beat a pillow without anyone knowing? Even if those around you would not understand, and you don't either, you must have some release before you explode.

Hostility sometimes can bring an emotional catharsis and it comes with sobs, tears, crying, screaming, and various visceral reactions. This is hard, taxing work and you have earned a breather. Do something physical after you record your insights or tentative insights. Please note your feelings, and do know you may be confused as to what you are feeling. It is part of your journey out of the wilderness. Be kind to yourself as you seek answers in the inner space of your being.

Inability to Do Normal Activities:
I Can't Go on This Way!

The inability to resume normal activities is negative concentration. It feels so good to feel bad, to steep ourselves in inertia, as we would steep a pot of tea. This happens in most grief events but is most noticeable when one moves to a retirement community, where all invitations are reused, photographs are fingered, and the desire to be miserable is paramount. Trying to relate to those who have no desire to relate causes us to be "weary in well-doing." As we remind ourselves that God is known in our relationships, we reach out and try again, even if we receive no emotional jelly beans in return. Knowing we should or ought to be up and about does not get us started; contrarily it adds to our general feeling that we can't do anything right. Such times of negative concentration zap our energy and accomplish zilch. It has been said that to learn to live and to learn to die is the same thing. The processes of grief are not the enemy, even if they feel like it.

Please move to your private, personal, special space, where you are crawling, scooting, and floundering in your own system's movement toward wholeness. Assure yourself of comfortable surroundings with your pen, pad, and tissues ready, and a tacit determination to ignore your telephone. If you find yourself yawning, please get up and move around. As you concentrate on breathing deeply, ask our Lord to be in your efforts to accept reality and deal with it creatively.

If you had to locate your apathy, where would you place it? Is it near your heart? In your limbs? In your gastrointestinal system? Does it feel as if your head is fuzzy and nonfunctional? If this were a physical symptom, where would you point? When I worked with very ill children, one little boy told me, "I hurt all over more than anyplace." Do you feel that also?

When is the last time you felt energy for anything? Are you excited when friends or family call or come by? Does your personal living space bring you any comfort? Does any food or

drink quench your thirst or assuage your hunger? Is this
blandness of existence something you have ever known before?
Do you feel you could just lie down and die? What other
times have you felt this way?

Is God at all real to you? What would it take for you to
feel God's love? Are you wanting a supernatural sign to prove
God's presence? Do you feel this unhappiness is what you
deserve? Why? Do you feel you have been treated so poorly
that God owes you something? Where does this thought
come from? Have you always felt you were special? Who
helped you to believe that was true?

Please stand and reach as high as you can. Breathe
deeply, reach again for the sky, and again be conscious of your
breath. Note how your breath comes and goes, almost without
effort. Jot a few notes about feelings and thoughts you
experienced during this time. Take a warm shower, noting the
feel of water as it caresses your skin. This journey is tedious
and energy draining, but the process will help you to be all
that God created you to be.

Social Sharing: "Now, with Me . . ."

The process of social sharing finds us still preoccupied with
our grief event. It seems we have a compelling need to talk
and think about, refer to, and tell again what happened. This
is not surprising when for many of us our loss is so catastrophic, it supersedes all else. Be it the loss of a deserved promotion, a long-distance move, loss of body function, divorce,
or death, we rehash the facts, the feelings, the innuendoes, the
before and after, and the ever-present paranoia. Sentences
begin, "Now, with me . . ." or "Before the surgeon arrived . . ."
or "Did I tell you what. . . ?" This social sharing is a needed
exercise. Without it we could get stuck in limbo, becoming
embittered, lonely, and alienated, believing everyone is shallow
and unsympathetic. There is a lovely Jewish custom still
practiced called a "meal of consolation." Family and friends

gather for a meal where the conversation is all about the deceased—the good, the not-so-good, the funny, as well as early and late remembrance. How good if small groups in church could convene after learning of divorce, serious illness, or an impending move for a meal of consolation.

Now pull apart from the world for some social sharing with your inner self. As you enter your private, secure place, have pad, pen, as well as tissues at hand, and ignore the intrusion of the phone or anyone at the door. Dialogue out loud, perhaps role-playing a scene you wish you could live again. Breathe a prayer for the gift of honesty without the varnish of "how I ought to feel."

Remember again the last time things were all right. Savor those memories. When did everything go wrong? What were you feeling at that time? Verbalize your feelings and share what you wish you might have said or changed. Have you told anyone about what you have just verbalized? Why not?

Now be honest as you ask yourself if you begin your sentences with the name of your loss. Have you felt people were bored by your constant repetition of events connected with your loss? Are you preoccupied with your loss? Are you interested in others' issues or events? Is your preoccupation with grief comfortable?

Do friends and family regularly invite you for outings? Have you attended any small group meetings at the suggestion of others? Why are you isolating yourself and concentrating your energy on the past? Could you host a lunch or dessert to mark a significant event you shared with the one you loved? A birthday, an anniversary, or a holiday event you have hosted in the past could be a time of laughing, crying, and remembering as all tell their special stories about the one who is no longer present. How sad if no one ever remembered our lives.

What are you feeling now? Did you catch a glimpse of yourself you are not happy with? How can you change that? What are you feeling—saddened, chagrined, excited, angered? Do you have a new plan for getting on with your life?

Jot down any insights or troubling questions to be dealt with at a later time. Arise, have a cool drink, eat a cracker, and know you have been engaged with a heavy agenda. Ask God to be with you in your continuing self-study as you explore your own inner space.

Rituals and Appeasements: Looking for Another Chance

With the death of one we loved, we give attention to physical checkups, making out a will, taking care of ourselves, and watching details. A person divorced may go on a rigid diet, undergo plastic surgery, or try an extreme exercise program. This is the time when we go through the photographs and write names and dates on the back, or balance our checkbooks scrupulously. Most of us need a nudge to get us through the tiresome and tedious events following a loss. The rituals we follow are not intrinsically negative, and may even be responsible actions, but it is helpful to know that they are an attempt on our part to achieve a second chance. If you have slipped back into the process of guilt, or never completed that process, you will have a greater compulsion to appease and try to make everything right. We may slip back into denial, feeling if we could just tie up all the loose ends, everything would be fine. Cleaning out closets, giving away possessions, holding a garage sale, or even buying a gravestone may be signs of our acceptance of the event, but often they are attempts to appease. How we long for another chance so that this time we can do it right. Good rituals help us get on with living our lives. They give us continuity and help us finish up unfinished business as we move through the process of grief.

I am sure you are weary, but in order to be all that God created you to be, it is time to pull again into your tranquil space to continue your self-study. By now you are well aware of the "drill." Enter into your journey into your own inner spaces. Close your eyes and lean back on the everlasting arms as you seek to be open to truth.

How has your life changed since your loss? What are you doing you never had to do before? What is the most difficult thing yet? Do you wonder, who dreamed up all these dreary details? Why did I not learn some of this before? It would have been so much easier to learn when there was someone to show me. I hate not having anyone to talk over decisions with. I don't need answers, but I do need to talk about all this that is strange and new.

What feels good about going through the books and papers of this one that is gone? Do you enjoy seeing the handwriting or reading marked passages, knowing they had meaning for him/her? What do you want to do with all these? Who would be excited to have books or periodicals on these issues? Are you afraid it will look as if you didn't care if you gave away those things? What was the feeling of the one who is gone concerning stewardship of belongings?

What feeling am I trying to appease with my rituals? Am I trying to appease God? Is God angry with me? Whom in my family am I trying to please? Do I need to ask forgiveness of someone? Am I angry at myself for somehow not being able to prevent this loss? Am I giving myself more power than I have?

This is a good time to begin a journal, even if you have never journaled before. Write as much or as little as you feel, although most of those who journal regularly will tell you they write more when things are not going well or when they are going exceptionally well. A journal is not shared except on a voluntary basis. It is a place where it is safe to confess fears, anxiety, depression, dreams, visions, and grandiose hopes. Start out with a new idea, observation, or insight. Talk about a problem of that day, or words or an idea that you read. Be honest as you look at yourself "warts and all." I like to go back from time to time to see what was troubling me or giving me joy. To journal gives me accountability, and an opportunity to reflect on that which I might ignore.

After looking at your pattern of rituals and appeasements, you now have the choice of deciding which rituals are productive and vital and which are time-consuming and needless. You are the one to choose. Write any new thoughts and give careful attention to what you are feeling. This would be a good time to take a walk or work in your garden. Be aware that you will not learn what you do not need to learn. Trust the process.

Hope: An Elusive Process

When we work through the processes of grief there is a gradual awakening of hope. We notice a fleeting thought things will be better. In time hope gradually comes more often than despair. It crosses our paths swiftly since it is not sure it is welcome. And it may not be, as we feel guilt for being happy. Survivor guilt causes us to be ashamed where our only fault is to be alive. It is easier to succumb to burnout and despair, but hope lets us learn from events so we are more knowledgeable, more humble, more human, and able to shake our "messiah complex." Is it not ironic that God created us human, and we try so hard to be God? There is hope with our children who grow and change and "return from the far country," and they are different and so are we. We find maturing even when we don't find agreement.

Those we love make mistakes. Some of their choices are not good. We wince at how others spend their money, but honesty forces us to admit our own mistakes, our own poor choices, our times of poor judgment, sometimes with money—and in the midst of our introspection we find hope. As we open ourselves to new situations and new relationships, hope comes more often than despair. We experience new opportunities for service and can delight in some change, rather than trying to keep everything "just as it was before." Hope becomes less mercurial and more of a reality. It could be because "not one bird stopped singing" that we experience hope once again.

With the process of hope we move easily to our special spot where we can continue our exploration of our inner self. We set our comforts, privacy, physical environment, and solitude, asking the Lord to be with us as we seek truth that sets us free.

When you exult in a bright spring day, do you feel twinges of guilt for being alive? Does the rest of the world seem to be getting on with life while you are marking time? Does your self-esteem seem quashed? Do you believe in yourself? Does it seem as if you are responsible for the whole world, and that everyone wants something from you? How long have you felt like this? Is this an old feeling or a new feeling? How can you change this?

Since your loss, have you made any new relationships? Have you signed up for a class to improve a skill or pursue a hobby? Can you cook creatively, or do you rely on your trusty can opener? Have you stretched your brain until you are tired of thinking? What are you going to do with the rest of your life? Where do you see hope? What do you have to do for this to happen?

Do you really believe that there is hope, and time will be on your side in experiencing it? Where does this belief come from? Who always talked with you about rainbows after storms, sunshine following rain, and God's grace even in the midst of despair? Do you feel God's presence, at least some of the time? What needs to happen for God's presence to be a reality more frequently? Do you know?

Now, as you bring this time to a close, taste the word "hope." What does it feel like on your tongue? Is it foreign or strange as you say it aloud? Do you want this to be a part of your life now, or does it feel disloyal to hope? Can you voice your uncertainty in a prayer, knowing that our loving and creative God, who knows us so well, loves us so well?

Write your findings and feelings, and go in hope.

Acceptance: All This?

This is the place we have been trying to reach. We are not the same as we were before; we cannot go back, for life is different, and we are different. In working through the processes of grief we have had to adjust to the realities and verities of life. Some days we want desperately to hold onto our past, for we know what it was like, and we have no assurance of what is to come. The challenge pulls at us to accept our loss and survive, or to sink in a featherbed of memories, obsessing over our loss, refusing to move on. Acceptance of reality, readjustment of priorities, and the integration of our loss has made us stronger. We are more sensitive to the hurts of others. We more readily accept life as a mixture of good and evil, and no longer do we tell others what they feel as we listen to their grief experience. We refrain from pushing our grief experience on others. The choices must be made, even if they are subtle. If we feel we should not ever have to adjust, we may be doomed to stay stuck in a morass, wondering why good things never happen to us. Not all our decisions will be perfect, and some will be costly in time and energy, but we will have begun the process of living—not just existing.

Go to your own sanctuary where you have pulled apart from the world to seek diligently the truth that so easily evades us. Sit relaxed as you look at your integration of life events, searching in your journey through the wilderness for growth and acceptance. Look to our living Lord for the peace needed as you dialogue internally.

Do you find yourself wanting to hold onto the past? If you let the past go, are you afraid there is nothing to take its place? Can you name your fear? Is it aging, health issues, loss of control, fear of not being loved? When you discover your fear, write it down, for unless we name it we cannot learn to live with it.

Since you have been involved in this self-study, do you feel more acceptance of what has happened to you? How has this changed your life? Do you hate adjustments and feel as if you have adjusted enough? Can we live without adjusting and compromising? Are you bitter or resentful that you have to adjust, but others do not?

What choices are ours as we come to this time of integrating? What has happened with what we have learned? Is integration of loss a part of the human condition? Have your values changed as you contemplate what you have endured? Is your relationship with God the same after the long, dark night of the soul, or is there a new depth in that relationship? Are you more real, less phony? Can you admit that you are not self-sufficient as you accept you are not in absolute control of your life?

This is the last of self-studies through the process of grief. You may want to go back and repeat some of the processes. Remembering that grief is not fixed and it will not be hurried, what do you need to do now? How will you use what you have learned as you have traveled into your inner self? Into the silence, into your waiting heart, ask again for God's presence.

Movement toward Wholeness

Grief is the spiritual reaction to being separated from what you have lost. Grief is not the enemy, but a system's process toward wholeness. We must be human enough to allow our grief, even when it makes others uncomfortable. We work at accepting reality, as little as we like it, but do our best to deal with it creatively. Some hymns will always bring tears to our eyes, and occasionally we choke up and can't sing, or a movie may have us dissolving in tears. It is embarrassing to cry in public, as we are so conditioned to show our emotions in private, but I hope we can affirm the rightness of an expression of grief within the fellowship of believers. Too long have we been brainwashed into identifying faith as stoic, no tears, stiff upper lip, and shoulder to the wheel. How absurd! Are we saying we never care enough about any person or any issue to show emotion? This certainly is not scriptural, but how many live as if it were.

So we sorrow not as those with no hope, we sorrow precisely as those who do! No matter how great our faith, we still need to cry, to ask questions, to express our rage, to doubt, and finally to doubt our doubts. "Blessed are those that mourn," not "Blessed are those that refrain from mourning." Where and how did we get these unrealistic pictures of grief? Our movies, television, books, and the media all give us a one-dimensional picture of grief. Grief liberates us to say "Yes" to life again. Bereavement is like psychological amputation, but a wounded spirit can and will heal with the analgesic of the grief process. Grief has so many faces and so many forms, but ultimately grief can be a part of the "abundant life" we are promised. And in that life, there is much singing.

Epilogue

It's autumn here in Kentucky, where all restraints are lifted, and the scarlet of the sumac vies with the gold of the sugar maple. This is an all-out display of bright orange and sunny yellow of varying shades. The elegant bronze, dull brown, and blue spruce and pines fill in the background. The skies are vivid blue with sunshine making days so perfect you want to bottle them. Then quickly, without warning, the cold front moves in, followed by gray, glucky days where the breathtaking magnificence of color swims in the gutter as rain falls day after day. Grayness seems to abound as we shiver in thin jackets, not yet willing to admit that winter is close. We know this is going to happen, but each fall we are surprised anew, somehow feeling cheated.

The parallel with our surprise at winter and our surprise with loss seems evident, but each time our reaction is fresh and compelling. We adapt quickly to the loss of small and insignificant things. But the shock at the loss of something or someone we truly loved tears at our hearts with a pervading sense of loneliness. An accompanying loss of control and a myriad of details combine to magnify our grief.

Even though it has been five years since my husband died, I continue to miss him. I miss sleeping spoon-fashion with him and the joy of waking up with him to face a new day. The last years when he was so sick found him growing weary as the daylight passed, but mornings were the time of day he greeted with contagious enthusiasm. How often I see or hear something I want to share with him. I miss talking things over with him. He really listened and could succinctly reframe my thoughts, usually going right to the heart of the matter. And I miss laughing with him. I not only loved this tall, dark man, I liked him. We married young, grew up together, and endured health crises and painful experiences. Sometimes we grew through heated discussions as we processed ideas and issues. But always we grew—together.

Of course I continue to miss what was such a good part of my life for so long. I struggle with my feelings of being cheated of some good years. But Harry will always be with me. He is in our children and grandchildren in their manner-isms, their senses of humor, their values, and their interests. He is present when our adult children or friends quote him or retell one of his stories. The yellow roses sent by friends on anniversaries are a nice reminder. Harry is with me in memory and in prayer, for the love between us is a spiritual bond that death did not sever.

Most of my questions have been resolved. I still have no idea what heaven is like. It remains a mystery, and that is all right as I have learned to live knowing there is much I will never understand this side of death. I am content knowing God is love, and it is in that love where heaven exists. I'm curious but content. While I do not have many answers, my journaling, my working with others who have questions, my writing, and my reading have brought acceptance even when I do not have understanding.

My mother is almost totally in a world of seventy or eighty years ago. This is better than the circumscribed sphere she actually inhabits, so we call it a blessing. She has good care, seems to feel little if any pain, is pleasant for the most part, and usually knows me and my sister. No longer do we try to dissuade her if she asks if we drove "that teams of bays" out to see her, or did we hang the wash out early, or if it is cold enough to butcher. That world is real to her, and we do not upset her by arguing. This is a time when being right is not a virtue if it angers or confuses her. She does not know her mar-velous mind only operates in the past. She remembers the jingles and the catchy little songs she taught us when we were very young but often introduces us to the health-care workers four times. I don't understand the why's of her life, but my anger has been worked through.

My house is for sale, as I am trying to simplify my way of living to preclude stairs, dust, molds, and yard work. There is grief in giving up my home with its treasure of memories; it has been my home for sixteen years, the longest I ever lived any place in my life. But houses do not make homes—that ability I will take with me to my new home. With God's help it will be a place of warmth and love where fellowship, fun, and food will be shared. Pragmatically I know that when I give up the security of places, grieving appropriately, then I am free to be aware of God's new challenges—and gifts.

I have a tendency to respond, when asked, that "I am fine." I have had some very good weeks. Unfortunately, I have also had a long stay in the hospital with pneumonia and face a long recuperation. Each time I am so ill I wonder if I will be able to return to the ministry I was called to. I try to live one day at a time and not worry ahead, and some days I do better than others. Adjusting is necessary on a daily basis. I am blessed with family and friends and I experience God's grace over and over. There are no easy answers, but where God is I can be content.

I have worked and continue to work to acknowledge my feelings, which are a testimony to my intense love and loss. They need time and space, and I must accept and embrace my feelings as normal, natural, and an integral part of my healing. Being open to the pain of a heart that seems to be broken allows God to enter its brokenness. One can exist with grief, or work through the process of grief, and I prefer the hard work and pain to bring me where I feel God wants me to be. For me, it is the way to the place where the birds never stop singing.

May God bless you in your quest for wholeness and meaning.

— DORIS MORELAND JONES
LOUISVILLE, KENTUCKY
APRIL 1997

About the Author

DORIS MORELAND JONES is the director of Middletown
United Methodist Counseling Center in Middletown,

Kentucky, as well as a
United Methodist clergy
member of the Kentucky
Annual Conference for
the last twenty-six years.
She has also served
as the director of the
Division of Ordained
Ministry for the General
Board of Higher Educa-
tion and Ministry in
Nashville, Tennessee, as
well as of counseling
centers in Indianapolis
and Louisville. Doris has
master's degrees in divinity and sacred theology. Her other
books include *Clergy Women: Problems and Satisfactions*, and
New Witnesses: United Methodist Clergy Women, both co-
authored with Harry Hale Jr. and Morton King.